Landscape of Fear

Landscape of Fear
Stephen King's
American Gothic

Tony Magistrale

With an Annotated Bibliography
Compiled by

Marshall B. Tymn

This book is dedicated to my father, Samuel,
and to my son, Christopher, with love and affection.

Contents

Preface

As I write these words, Stephen King's latest novel, *It*, has sold over 1.5 million hardcover editions at $22.95 per copy. The novel has maintained its position at the top of *The New York Times* best seller list since its release ten weeks ago. For those readers who already savor the quality of King's fiction, the achievement of *It* comes as no real surprise; the author has earned both his reputation and money. But there are others who remain highly skeptical of King's enormous success. This latter group is confident that he will never be more than a hack writer preying upon the tasteless sensibilities of a popular audience that equates a meal at McDonald's with dining at a gourmet restaurant.

I wrote *Landscape of Fear: Stephen King's American Gothic* for each of the groups I have described above. For those millions of readers who are drawn to King because his tales are engaging or terrifying or both, I offer this book as a vehicle for understanding and appreciating his fiction even more. If I have been successful in this effort, perhaps a new aspect of King's creative imagination will be illuminated, or maybe my readers will view King's work in a different context after discovering what I have to say about him. At any rate, this analysis was never meant as a "reader's guide" to Stephen King; I believe Douglas Winter's fine book *Stephen King: The Art of Darkness* handles that task better than I could ever hope. If there is a core liability to Winter's approach, however, it is that he must often sacrifice analyses of unity and depth in favor of tracing the broad sweep of King's prolific canon. On at least one level of being, then, my book seeks to fill this gap by deliberately restricting its scope to the major themes and recurring patterns found in King's fiction.

Since my first exposure to King's work in the paperback edition of *Carrie*, which I read when it was first published, I have maintained that what is most horrifying in his tales has less to do with prehistoric creatures roaming the night or vampires cruising for nourishment. Rather, his deepest terrors are sociopolitical in nature, reflecting our worst fears about vulnerable western institutions—our governmental bureaucracies, our school systems, our communities, our familial relationships. In other words, King writes about horrors that operate on a variety of levels—embracing the literal as well as the symbolic. In his essay "The Pleasure of the Subtext: Stephen King's Id-Life Crisis," Andrew Klavan goes as far to insist that not only do "King's works have a subtext, but that the subtext is all they have" (46). Indeed, while King depicts active, and often malevolent, supernatural occurrences, these forces usually require some degree of human involvement: the real menace of the supernatural is that it attacks whenever and wherever the human mind is most susceptible. King forces us to contemplate issues that few of us can bear to consider directly for any length of time. As Douglas Winter reminds us in his essay "The Funhouse of Fear,"

> The monsters of our times are less exotic and, discouragingly, more symptomatic than their predecessors. A soulless insanity sparks the finest horror novel of the Eighties, Thomas Harris's *Red Dragon*. Child abuse is the relentless theme of the best-selling novels of V.C. Andrews, while the dissolution of family and marriage haunts the fiction of Charles L. Grant. The curses of socialization—notably, venereal disease—infect the films of David Cronenberg and the fiction of Clive Barker. Urban decay is the insistent background of Ramsey Campbell's short stories. (16)

King's fiction is at the center of this contemporary emphasis on the sociology of horror. His work acknowledges that we are not immune to the technological mistakes which occur even in a far-off town whose name we have never heard before; that the securities of our personal microcosms—our homes and communities—no longer represent effective sanctuaries against the chaos of an ever-changing, ever-narrowing larger world. These are the concerns he brings to our attention in his best work, and if at times he slips into the merely grotesque or the sensational, it is the price he pays for venturing into such dangerous territory.

It is in light of these very real contemporary issues that I now address those critics of Mr. King who have either rejected his work because of what they have heard about it (since they refuse to read it themselves), and those, who, after reading one or two of his novels, have dismissed the writer because he supposedly lacks the seriousness of purpose required of good literature.

Consider, for example, Walter Wager's scathing review of *It*, recently published in *The New York Times Book Review:*

> Where did Stephen King, the most experienced crown prince of darkness, go wrong with *It*? Almost everywhere. Casting aside discipline, which is as important to a writer as imagination and style, he has piled just about everything he could think of into this book and too much of each thing as well. (9)

Wager's attack reflects the usual litany of critical complaints directed against King, and it is clear, from interviews, lectures, and his smarting return shots in *Danse Macabre*, that King is as disappointed with his critics as they are with him. My own sympathies are usually with Mr. King, as I often wonder why reviewers such as Walter Wager are so reluctant to emphasize what King does *right* in his novels, instead of always circling back to his perceived liabilities.

There is little doubt that King's enormous popularity has damaged his reputation among academicians and literary scholars. There is a disquieting tendency among many English teachers and intellectuals in this country to view themselves as the final arbiters of "high culture," and any artist, regardless of his or her talent, threatens that exclusive *sanctum sanctorum* if s/he seeks admittance with a large, popular audience in tow. As long as John Irving remained an obscure and impoverished novelist in the production of several fine early books, his academic reputation was secured. But once he published *The World According to Garp* and gained an enormously popular following, he was immediately susceptible to the kind of critical hostility King has been receiving for years. It is interesting that the only real exceptions to this maxim appear to be authors such as Bernard Malamud, John Barth, and Saul Bellow—all extremely popular but also acceptable to English department curricula. Perhaps their dual achievements are related to their willingness to keep within the academies either as teachers or as chroniclers of academic life.

It would do well for King's detractors to consider him in Dickensian terms, for King shares much in common with the English novelist: his fecundity, his sprawlingness, his creation of grotesque characters and distinctive speech, his vivid animation of setting and place, but most of all, his enormous mass

4   **Landscape of Fear**

popularity. As King himself reminds us in an address he delivered
on November 6, 1986 at the University of Maine, Orono,

The novel is quite well. What we should perhaps be moaning over is the
death of literary criticism in America, the loss of clear, sane voices in the
popular periodicals in our time, the snobbishness of those writers who analyze
fiction for the small and oppressive, and the really alarming failure of these
would-be critics to distinguish between quality and celebrity. To go even
a step further, I would suggest a stranger inability: the inability to see that
quality and celebrity need not always be mutually exclusive.

Certainly King employs the themes and conventions of a
much maligned genre, but his best work does so with a literary
sophistication and level of quality equal to that of anyone writing
today. The very concept of "high" versus "popular" culture seems
besides the point. The deconstructionists (with their focus on
the sub-texts of fiction) and current textual critics have helped
to change the scope of contemporary critical approaches to
literature. And now several voices have even begun to
acknowledge what writers like Leslie Fiedler have maintained
for years: that to be good, literature does not necessarily need
to remain outside the realm of popular acceptance.

The author wishes to acknowledge the assistance of the
following individuals who helped to make this book possible.
First, at the University of Vermont, Professors Michael Stanton,
Virginia Clark, Margaret Edwards, and Dean Frank Manchel read
and commented upon this manuscript at length. Their expertise
and support is everywhere apparent. I also wish to thank my
father, Samuel, to whom this book is co-dedicated, for his editorial
suggestions throughout the composing process. I would likewise
be remiss if I failed to include my gratitude to Professor Ken
Wagner for his excellent introduction, to Professor Marshall
Tymn for his comprehensive bibliography, to Professors Burton
Hatlen and Kirk Vaughan at the University of Maine, Orono,
for sharing their counsel and recollections of life with Stephen
King when the latter was their student, to Greg Weller, Alan
Cohen, Norman and Kay Tederous and Brian Kent for their many
interdisciplinary suggestions, and to my wife, Jennifer, for
providing me with the patience and encouragement necessary
to complete this project.

Finally, this book would not resemble its current shape were
it not for the assistance of the University of Vermont
undergraduates in English 261, a senior seminar on the work
of Stephen King—to my knowledge, the first course ever offered

at any university dealing exclusively with King's fiction. The enthusiasm of the students in this class was equalled only by their critical expertise, and I am grateful to all 19 of them for providing me with a classroom forum for presenting and refining many of the ideas found between these covers. Mr. King was close to the truth when, upon being introduced to several of these students, he pronounced that "you must know my work better than me." The author also thanks Stephen King himself for his gentle encouragement throughout the writing of this book and, most of all, for his forgiveness for whatever liberties I have taken with his fiction.

Sections of this book were originally published elsewhere. A version of Chapter 2 appeared in *The Journal of Popular Literature*, while a version of Chapter 5 originally appeared in *Extrapolation*. My thanks to the editors of both journals, Ray Browne and Tom Clareson, for providing me with these early opportunities to expose my theories to a scholarly audience.

Tony Magistrale
Burlington, Vermont
January, 1988

Introduction

Good literature has the power to reveal in dramatic form what social scientists seek to analyze and explain. The outstanding contribution of Magistrale's work is the connection between the horror of Stephen King's fiction and the prevailing social conditions of contemporary American culture. Magistrale's analysis of King's novels and tales undercuts a popular perception that King is merely the author of macabre stories which shock and excite the emotions of a reading public in search of sensation. While King's enormous commercial success and his literary detractors both suggest that the writer is not to be taken very seriously, Magistrale argues the converse: that King's fiction, to be understood accurately, must be viewed as contemporary social satire, revealing collective cultural fears and fantasies which go unspoken in everyday life. Thus, the horror of King's fiction mirrors the current maladies of our social relationships.

The major corpus of Stephen King's work is a critique of the ways in which the dignity of the individual is assaulted and corrupted by self-interest, powerlessness, and a dependency on bureaucratic and technological authority. This assault can be fruitfully explicated in terms of the contemporary narcisstic concern for the self. Therefore, before attempting to interpret King's fiction in light of this sociological context, I must first provide a brief description of what is meant by the concept of social narcissism.

The narcissistic concern with the self is fostered by discontent with institutions. Survey research (see Davis, 1980) and diverse social theorists such as Habermas (1973) and Lasch (1979) have claimed that the contemporary breakdown in the authority of American institutions has contributed to a general attitude of social cynicism and despair. Disrespect for the authority of institutions reflects the popular perception of the government as corrupt, of the schools as a place where children learn only about violence and dope, and of the family as a "haven" that is slowly collapsing.

Social discontent, however, is not by itself an example of narcissism. What is an expression of narcissism is the prevailing cultural response to this dissatisfaction. Discontent, coupled with the conviction that this society cannot change, fosters sole concern for the self. In other words, social despair can atrophy into narcissism. The failure of institutions to promote satisfying social experiences results in individuals believing that personal survival is the only realistic goal. Christopher Lasch argues convincingly in his book *The Culture of Narcissism* that survivalism has become the dominant ideology of contemporary culture. Individuals with little hope for a better society find it difficult to make the commitments necessary to alter the social conditions of their lives. Self-fulfillment is viewed as a product of one's own struggle to change personally, rather than as the result of changing society. In this context changing personally means, in effect, to adapt to social conditions of institutional decline by learning how to "cope." Consequently, people today expect less from their society, yet more from themselves. In other words, people want a better life without wanting equally a better society.

In a narcisstic culture, freedom is defined in terms of one's ability to survive the pitfalls of society by escaping from the evil assumed to be endemic to social life. Magistrale highlights the *real* evils in King's world by focusing on his fictional portraits of contemporary social conditions—the ways in which this society undermines the morality necessary for love, of self and for others. King's fiction echoes a dominant concern of many contemporary social scientists: the lack of community and social connectedness in American society, and the culture's general spirit of apathy.

In his most optimistic moments, King appeals to a public in search of a way out of this wasteland. His child-adults and the bonds they share among themselves in defiance of society attempt to re-capture the legitimacy of human feeling trivialized by both the logic of bureaucratic control and the values of materialism. King's ultimate interest is with individuals and their personal struggles to transcend the corrupting influences of society. Jack Sawyer, the central character in *The Talisman*, for example, is in permanent flight from the social forces representing both the Territories and the United States. Like other popular rebels, Luke Skywalker in *Star Wars* and the children in *E.T.*, many of King's characters (especially his children) resist the prevailing values of society which de-humanize the individual by making love and community problematic. Luke Skywalker and the children of *E.T.* taught us that we must trust our own feelings in distinguishing good from evil. The "evil empire" could only be destroyed and E.T. saved from the "authorities" by children who rejected the credibility of bureaucratic power and technological superiority. Like these other heroes of popular culture, King's protagonists suggest to us that social authority ought to be based on other values.

Many of King's young people—Ben Mears in *'Salem's Lot*, Danny Torrance in *The Shining*, Charlie McGee in *Firestarter*, and Jack Sawyer in *The Talisman*—rebel against the social institutions of America. And their refusal to comply with the conformity requested of them by the various representatives of these institutions brands them as outlaws. Therefore, to survive they must create new social identities and interpersonal relationships. These protagonists, among others, participate in what Magistrale defines as a "moral flight to freedom." Insofar as King's young heroes and heroines are always seen fleeing from a variety of social commitments and institutions, his fiction can be read as a dramatization of contemporary cultural narcissism. As Magistrale contends, the only way for King's characters to resist the existing societal assault on the self is to abandon the society altogether, by departing in small interpersonal groups. Such collective resistance appears necessary as the only avenue available for moral endurance.

The collective form of small group rebellion portrayed in King's work is therefore different from the more popular types of deviance in contemporary America, which is more likely to take the form of *individual* withdrawal. Individuals in modern America appear to be responding to their society's failures by spending more time developing coping strategies—from getting into better physical shape to drugs. Such a retreat is, of course, self-defeating. The self can never be an exit for discontent. Contentment with life requires better social relationships which, in turn, shape our personal experiences.

Although King's heroes rebel against a solipsistic retreat to the self, they do not directly challenge the society their rebellion rejects. The original founders of the Free Zone community in *The Stand*, for example, engage in a form of collective escape from mainstream America that is similar to the "hippie" move to the communes in the 1960s and the appeal of religious cults in the 1970s. King's rage against the horrors of American society notwithstanding, the political effect of the journey to Colorado in this novel is not the creation of an enduring alternative society; as soon as the Boulder community expands its membership, it begins once again to embody the values of pre-plague America. Worse yet, those remaining members of this community who recall its origins—notably, Frannie and Stu—offer no resistance to the political changes which are occurring. Their decision to leave Boulder and go to Maine reflects their feelings of social impotence; they are essentially continuing the flight from any commitment to political engagement.

Frannie and Stu are instructive representatives of King's canon, as their pattern of escape is repeated by many other characters. But if these moral heroes and heroines possess the courage to leave society, why can't they summon the courage to change society? The answer appears to be that King does not believe the individual can effectively confront the social forces he detests. Ultimately, the lack of political confrontation with the forces of evil King portrays in society reifies such evil while disguising the psychology of escapism in the moral rhetoric of rebellion.

In spite of King's concern for a new community, the majority of his men and women seem motivated by their individual contempt for the present. The problem within their wholesale rejection of society, however, is that the building of a new community requires a shared political vision of an alternative society. King's characters reflect the ideology of individualism in that morality is defined exclusively in terms of one's own ability to struggle against evil, to remain moral in the face of immoral social circumstances. Consequently, life becomes simply an ethical test of endurance with character the criterion for a salvation which will free the self from the horrors of life. I reject such a philosophy, as I believe that greater freedom for individuals requires political actions that enhance the greater morality of society.

The fact that Magistrale's analysis of Stephen King can lead us to discover and debate such important political and philosophical issues gives concrete meaning to the lesson of hermeneutics. Regardless of the intent of King's fiction, Professor Magistrale leads his readers through the web of King's horror, all the while illuminating the connection between the fantasy of our imagination and the predicament of our present social experience. Questions such as where King stands politically and why the horror in his fiction is relevant to his politics can only

be knowledgeably addressed by those fortunate enough to have
read the contents of this book.

Kenneth S. Wagner
Hamilton College
December 1986

Chapter 1
Toward Defining an American Gothic:
Stephen King and the
Romance Tradition

In a recent edition of my favorite comic strip, "Bloom County," Opus, the obtuse penguin, suffers from a severe case of amnesia. Unable to remember even the most elemental aspects of his personality, he wonders aloud, "Do I prefer spinach salads for lunch?...or pistachio-nut ice cream? Do I read Saul Bellow or Stephen King?" The final frame shows Opus at home in a comfortable chair, dipping into a gallon tub of pistachio-nut ice cream and reading an enormous book entitled *The Gore* by Stephen King.

Perhaps better than any other comic strip currently in circulation, "Bloom County" achieves its humor in reflecting and parodying the manners of American popular culture. In the particular episode cited above, pistachio-nut ice cream and the brand-name fame of Stephen King are emblematic of America's junk food culture, while Saul Bellow is paired with the more respectable spinach salad. As the confused Opus acknowledges, pistachio-nut ice cream and Mr. King are clearly distinguished from the more substantial contents available in spinach salads and the fiction of Saul Bellow. King's novels may be more fun to devour than those of Bellow, but they are also perceived as being less significant, less "serious."

Despite an emerging corpus of film and literary criticism in the past few years that has treated King's fiction quite seriously, his long-standing artistic reputation is still considered in doubt. There are several reasons for this, the most frequently ascribed of which probably fall within this list:

(1) King makes too much money with his books (at this writing his yearly income is greater than the gross national products of most third world nations) and any popular writer can't be so good as his press;

(2) he produces nearly a book a year, so he must not work very hard at his craft;

(3) his predominant subject themes are the supernatural, the bizarre, and the occult, and he is therefore only tangentially concerned with the realities of contemporary life; and

(4) he needs an editor, presumably because many of his books are overwritten and badly organized.

It should not suffice for an *aficionado* of King's work to dismiss the above points as merely the cynical judgement of English teachers who are underpaid and unimpressed by creatures of the night. King himself has, to varying degrees, addressed each of these complaints in interviews, introductions to his fiction, and in his own analysis of the horror genre, *Danse Macabre*. In all honesty, much of King's *oeuvre* would benefit from the tough advice of a good editor; there are, for example, a number of instances where King's work could be substantially improved as a result of some judicious revising. However, it is both unfair and inaccurate when any or all of these laments serve as the basis for degrading King's importance as a serious American artist. Indeed, one of the primary motivations for the existence of this book is the resolute commitment on the part of its author to enhance the literary reputation—which, as we have seen, is often at odds with a popular one—of Stephen King's fiction by giving it the type of analysis it justly deserves, and for too long has failed to enjoy.

1

Who buys Stephen King's books and why?

In discussing the influence of the sociopolitical atmosphere of the 1950s on the evolution of the horror film, King argues in *Danse Macabre* that his generation represented

...fertile ground for the seeds of terror, we were war babies; we had been raised in a strange circus atmosphere of paranoia, patriotism, and national *hubris*. We were told that we were the greatest nation on earth and that any Iron Curtain outlaw who tried to draw down on us in that great saloon of international politics would discover who the fastest gun in the west was (as in Pat Frank's illuminating novel of the period, *Alas, Babylon*), but we were also told exactly what to keep in our fallout shelters and how long we would have to stay in there after we won the war. We had more to eat than any nation in the history of the world, but there were traces of Strontium-90 in our milk from nuclear testing. (23)

None of the issues King discusses above has changed much in three decades; the stakes are still high, the missiles more plentiful. The anxiety associated with the realities of modern life leads readers to King. His apocalyptic vision of a world in ruins (*The Stand*) or the nightmare of science unleashed beyond mortal control (*Firestarter, The Mist,* and "I am the Doorway") are invented themes bordering on the very edge of possibility. The parallels between the world of King's novels and our own grow increasingly striking as we spin blindfolded toward the twenty first century. In an age where it sometimes seems that to eat and drink and breathe is to be helplessly inviting cancer; where the constant threat of war in the Middle East and Latin America threatens to escalate into one final conflagration; where instruments of mass destruction increase in capability and sophistication, while those in charge of them seem less responsible and prudent; and where random and purposeless acts of violence have tacitly become an accepted element of Western life, King's fictional plots are appearing less and less surreal. And whether his audience reads to indulge a kind of perverse enchantment in imagining the destruction of humankind, or reads to reaffirm the importance of circumventing Armageddon, King's novels and tales are reminders of how far we as a collective society and culture have strayed from a balanced moral perspective. As a result, his fiction possesses a political and social relevance that is as serious and significant a contribution as anything Saul Bellow has yet to tell us.

King's tendency toward overwriting notwithstanding, his prose style remains deceptively simple and accessible, and the ease with which one of his imaginary worlds envelops the reader represents another reason for his popularity. In reading a novel such as *The Shining* or *Christine*, it is quite possible to withdraw from all commitments to family and friends, re-emerging after two or three days bleary-eyed and perhaps slightly paranoid, but nonetheless aware of having been transported into a fascinating realm. King himself acknowledges this very tendency in an interview he shared with Douglas Winter published in the book *Faces of Fear:*

In most cases, [my] characters seem very open and accessible. They seem like people that you would like to know, or even people you *do* know. People respond to that, and there is very little of that in novels today.... In most of the books, I think, there's a kind of Steve King hammock that you fall into—and you feel really comfortable in that hammock, because you know these people and you feel good about them. You don't have unease about who they are; you have unease about the circumstances that they find themselves in. And that's where the suspense comes from. (251)

King's best work employs many of the same techniques found in film, which is the most obvious explanation why his novels translate so well into movies. He possesses the ability to maintain levels of suspense because the imaginary world he portrays is so accurately visual. Consider, for example, this scene from the short story "The Ledge," a tale in which a jealous husband, who has discovered his wife's infidelity, torments her lover by forcing him to walk around the penthouse ledge of a high-rise apartment building:

> I waited for the wind to drop, but for a long time it refused to, almost as though it were Cressner's willing ally. It slapped against me with vicious, invisible fingers, prying and poking and tickling. At last, after a particularly strong gust had made me rock on my toes, I knew that I could wait forever and the wind would never drop all the way off.
> So the next time it sank a little, I slipped my right foot around and, clutching both walls with my hands, made the turn. The crosswind pushed me two ways at once, and I tottered. For a second I was sickeningly sure that Cressner had won his wager. Then I slid a step farther along and pressed myself tightly against the wall, a held breath slipping out of my dry throat. (190)

In this excerpt we see King's descriptive abilities at their very best. Not only does the reader clearly visualize the desperate plight of the narrator, clinging to the building with his legs and hands while the wind's personified "fingers" pull at his body, but his terrifying situation likewise fills us with pity and fear. As his journey around the building unfolds, his staccato breaths become our's, until finally we urge his survival, completely overlook his infidelity with Cressner's wife, and applaud the ironic conclusion as the narrator turns the tables on his tormentor and makes him walk the ledge.

King's many skills and liabilities as a writer are readily apparent. But his name has been elevated to brand-name status primarily because of his ability to create supernatural effects. As I will argue elsewhere in this book, I believe these extraordinary occurrences can be traced directly to King's sociopolitical perspective on contemporary America, but this is probably not an affiliation most readers make. As is the case with his general prose style, King's monsters are always highly visual manifestations—whether they occupy the form of rampaging trucks on an interstate highway, a malevolent deity who inhabits the cornfields of Nebraska, or the animated topiary outside a Colorado hotel. Once the reader is introduced to these creatures, he sleeps the worst for it.

King's most loyal readers belong to generations of movie goers who have attended repeated viewing of Lucas' *Star Wars* trilogy, adults and children who were nurtured on television reruns of *The Twilight Zone* and *The Outer Limits*, individuals who have spent entire afternoons transfixed by the human-animal-vegetable hybrids in the paintings of Hieronymus Bosch, and those whose literary tastes remain committed to annual readings of Tolkien's *Lord of the Rings Trilogy*. Several critics, most notably Douglas Winter and Don Herron, have reminded us of King's debt to the book and film success of *Rosemary's Baby* and *The Exorcist*. In the early 1970s these productions revitalized public fascination with the horror genre by focusing on its urban possibilities. Steering deliberately away from the science-fiction backdrops that characterized the genre's major contribution to literature and film in the 1950s and 1960s, Ira Levin's *Rosemary's Baby* and William Blatty's *The Exorcist* bring the terror back down to earth; indeed, their work is a reminder that the darkest evils are always those found in our neighborhoods, in our children, and in ourselves rather than in some deserted place out among the stars. As King reminds us in *Danse Macabre*, "the strongest watchspring of *Rosemary's Baby* isn't the religious subtheme but the book's use of urban paranoia.... Our dread for Rosemary springs from the fact that she seems the only normal person in a whole city of dangerous maniacs" (288-9).

King not only capitalized on the immeasurable public interest awarded to *Rosemary's Baby* and *The Exorcist*, as both novels and film adaptations appeared just before King's first publication (*Carrie*, 1974), but he likewise continued to emphasize the horror potential available in the everyday world. King's monsters are found not on planets light years away or in other exotic or foreign locations. Instead, they inhabit the groundfloors of American factories, high schools, and rectories. Some of his creatures prowl the dark recesses of woods and swamps, but his most frightening creations can be found in neighborhood communities occupying positions of power and authority or in Washington controlling the fate of the nation. Like *Rosemary's Baby* and *The Exorcist*, King's world is an easily recognizable one, and when terror is unleashed in that world it becomes all the more terrifying because we comprehend its immediate relevance to our daily lives.

2

It is his awareness of the pervasiveness of evil—indeed, that it exists in ourselves, our social and political institutions, in short, in everything human—that links King to the literary tradition of American gothicism. In his essay "King and the Literary Tradition of Horror and the Supernatural," Ben Indick argues that King "has absorbed and utilized those qualities which characterize the different types of stories in the horror genre. In his own distinctive style are mirrored the major traditions he has inherited" (175). While Indick broadly outlines those gothic elements which have influenced King (e.g. the ghost story, vampire tale, etc.), he pays scant attention to the American romance tradition of the nineteenth century. Although he briefly includes mention of Poe in his analysis, Indick does not provide any thorough investigation linking King to Poe and other American writers from the nineteenth century. In fact, King owes as much to this earlier generation of writers—particularly Hawthorne and Twain—as he does to any German vampire legend or to his literary contemporaries, Blatty and Levin. The connection between King and the nineteenth century requires a critical forum for several reasons. The most important is by way of establishing King's place in the mainstream tradition of American literature. At the same time this relationship can also provide an appropriate context for discussing the origins of King's moralist vision.

The most obvious similarity that King shares with these nineteenth-century writers is his reliance on gothic settings and atmospheric techniques. Poe's haunted houses, Hawthorne's symbolic forests, and Melville's assorted workplace dungeons each bring to mind respectively *The Shining*, *Pet Sematary*, and "Graveyard Shift."

In Poe's tales of fantasy and terror, confined atmospheric environments are representative of the narrator's or main character's circumscribed state of mind. Thus, Prince Prospero's proud egotism in "The Masque of the Red Death" is illustrated by his seven-chambered castle sealed off from the world by metal doors and thick stained glass windows; the narrator's mental anguish in "The Pit and the Pendulum" is reflected in his dark, gradually narrowing prison cell; and similarly, the Usher mansion is emblematic of Roderick Usher's mental status: both its interior apartments and external facade exist in a state of chaos and disintegration.

The jump from Poe to King is really more of a skip, as their protagonists often find themselves in similar claustrophobic circumstances. In Poe's fiction, as Frederick Frank points out in his essay "The Gothic Romance," "Place becomes personality, as every corner and dark recess exudes a remorseless aliveness and often a vile intelligence" (14). King likewise employs physical settings as a mirror to a character's psychological condition, and *The Shining, 'Salem's Lot*, "Graveyard Shift," "Strawberry Spring," "The Boogeyman," and "The Raft" are his most instructive examples. His gothic landscapes are animated by a terrible potency that appears out of all proportion to the small and vulnerable humans who are held within its bondage. Like Poe's buildings, King's architecture is imbued with a life of its own, an unnatural biology that reflects the character and history of its former inhabitants.

Although *The Shining* contains several explicit allusions to "The Masque of the Red Death," the Overlook's real inspiration is the Usher house, replete with its legacy of sin and death as well as its ultimate destruction. And similar to Poe's descriptions of the decayed mansion's relationship to its owner, the interior of King's Overlook hotel—with its dark, twisting corridors and infamous history—reflects Jack Torrance's own psyche. At the end of *The Shining* Torrance could no more depart from the Overlook than Usher could abandon the crumbling mansion that becomes his tomb.

Hawthorne's woods are a place of spiritual mystery; in them, young Goodman Brown, Reuben Bourne, and minister Arthur Dimmesdale must confront their own darkest urges. In *Pet Sematary*, Hawthorne's historical sense of puritanical gloom associated with the forest is mirrored in King's ancient Micmac Indian burial ground. Dr. Louis Creed, like so many of Hawthorne's youthful idealists, discovers in the Maine woods that evil is no mere abstraction capable of being manipulated or ignored. Instead, he finds his own confrontation with evil to be overwhelming, and like Hawthorne's Ethan Brand and Goodman Brown, he surrenders to its vision of chaos and corruption.

Melville's fiction, whether set on the sea or in the urban office, describes the quiet nightmare of a capitalist economic structure devoid of humanitarian principles. The workplace as torture chamber is one of Melville's most frequent themes, and it is a vision that informs fiction as diverse as "Bartleby the Scrivner," *Benito Cereno*, and *Moby Dick*. The crew on board Ahab's *Pequod*, for example, is cajoled into blood oaths that force them to relinquish their humanity, becoming mere extensions of their mad employer's quest for personal revenge against Moby Dick. King's descriptions of work experience in contemporary America bear close similarities to Melville's: in "Graveyard Shift," "Trucks," and "The Mangler," his characters are forced to perform labor under similar dehumanizing conditions. For both Melville and King, gothic settings and apparatus are often evoked as vehicles for underscoring a sterile and rotting economic system.

Melville's urban and sea scapes and Poe's claustrophobic interiors make their regional influences difficult to pinpoint. Their use of gothic settings, while always specific and important to theme, could conceivably take place anywhere in the world; in Melville's sea novels and Poe's *Narrative of Arthur Gordon Pym*, for example, the macrocosmic backdrop of the ocean, because of its sheer enormity, floats the reader in a sort of salt water vacuum. Hawthorne, on the other hand, was at his best as a regionalist author. His sense of Massachusetts—as a repository for historical events as well as a physical entity—is intrinsic to his most important fiction. Hawthorne's New England forests and puritan ancestry function as living beings in his work; they are always subject to his closest scrutiny, and often exert a profound influence over the lives of his protagonists.

At the Conference for the Fantastic in Arts, held in 1984 at Boca Raton, Florida, I asked Stephen King, who delivered the conference's main address, what effect living in Maine had produced on his writing. He replied that "there's a Maine very few outsiders ever get to know. It's a place of rich Indian lore, rocky soil that makes it difficult to grow things, and incredible levels of poverty. Once you get out from behind the coastal resorts, the real Maine begins." King's Maine is a place of terrifying loneliness where nature seems antagonistic to human habitation and where men and women often feel the same degree of estrangement from one another as they do toward the supernatural creatures who threaten their lives. Burton Hatlen, perhaps the most persuasive critic on the regional influence on King, argues in "Beyond the Kittery Bridge: Stephen King's Maine," that in the writer's "myth of Maine," characters are confronted "with an overwhelming, terrifying challenge, and they won't survive it unless they can find within themselves some kind of courage that they didn't know they had" (59).

King is a regionalist in much the same way that Hawthorne was; each sensed that the real meanings behind the history and physical textures of a particular place could be fathomed only after great study—and what better laboratory than one's own ancestral past and regional legacy? Thus, *The Scarlet Letter* or "Young Goodman Brown" can no more be separated from their distinct puritan Massachusetts backgrounds than King's *'Salem's Lot* or *Pet Sematary* can be extricated from contemporary Maine.

King captures the native speech patterns, the local raw materials of a cold climate, and the specificity of place that set his readers firmly in a rural Maine world. His north country is a region of a particular people, language, and customs, all set apart by an awareness of their differences from cities even as near as Boston. King returns over and over to descriptions of his native state, and he does so for some of the same purposes Hawthorne used in writing about Massachusetts: each author understands that the universal themes of great literature—human sin, fear, and endurance—can only be rendered truthfully within settings and by personalities an artist has come to know on a first-hand basis. Much as Hawthorne relied on puritan New England as a setting to describe the foibles and sins that are the inheritance of humankind, King views Maine as a deliberate backdrop for his own allegories, enabling him to utilize specific elements from that culture in his portrayal of the moral conflicts common to us all.

3

In his book *The American Novel and Its Tradition*, Richard Chase defines the most important aspects of the romance tradition:

Astonishing events may occur, and these are likely to have a symbolic or ideological, rather than a realistic, plausibility. Being less committed to the immediate rendition of reality than a novel, the romance will more freely veer toward mythic, allegorical, and symbolistic forms. (13)

Chase makes these points with reference to the work of Hawthorne and Melville, but it is immediately apparent, even from what has been said only so far in this opening chapter, that the description also applies just as well to King. Indeed, as we shall see, the use of the horror story as sociopolitical allegory is one of King's major contributions to the genre. Like King, the nineteenth century possessed a similar interest in portraying the discovery of self through metaphors of motion, the journey quest, and the conflict between ideologically opposing forces. "William Wilson," *The Narrative of Arthur Gordon Pym*, "Young Goodman Brown," "Ethan Brand," "My Kinsman Major Molineux," *The Marble Faun, Moby-Dick*, and *The Adventures of Huckleberry Finn* represent a blend of the literal with the symbolic, realism with allegory, and thus maintain certain similarities to King's canon.

The strength of King's stories is probably not to be found, however, in Melville's philosophical contemplations, nor in Poe and Hawthorne's speculations regarding the relationship between art and life. But the tentative and often precarious moral search for selfhood that characterizes the nineteenth-century romance tradition is likewise present in King. King's world-view is based on the complexity of modern life, and his protagonists begin the voyage toward moral wholeness only after experiencing the most disturbing encounters with evil. King relies on the journey motif in *The Stand, The Talisman, Pet Sematary*, and *Thinner* for the same reasons the nineteenth century did: the literal voyage—be it westward across contemporary America, downstream on the Mississippi River, or into the mysterious woods of a New England forest—becomes a metaphor for the journey into the self. This journey is fraught with danger along the way because King's young protagonists, like those of Twain and Hawthorne, learn that true moral development is gleaned only from a struggle with the actual, from confronting the dark legions of Morgan Sloat and Randall Flagg, rather than by avoiding them.

King writes fiction from the perspective of a fallen human world, and his characters commence their voyage to a moral comprehension of this world only at the very point where they become profoundly aware of the pervasive existence of evil. In Poe, Melville, Hawthorne and Twain, no individual is immune from the lure of evil—indeed, many of their characters succumb to its attractiveness and commit the most despicable acts of depravity. For example, neither Poe nor Melville satisfactorily explains why the narrators of "The Tell Tale Heart" and "The Black Cat" hate the old man and the cat, or why Captain Ahab feels the need to indulge his anger toward a white whale. However, there is strong suggestion that Ahab and Poe's narrators secretly hate what they see to be a reflection of themselves found in the objects of their vengeance; for it is clear that in abandoning the most fundamental precepts of morality in order to accomodate the selfish urge to dominate and torment their fellow creatures, Ahab and Poe's narrators end up destroying themselves. Most of the other central protagonists from the canons of Poe, Hawthorne, and Melville are measured by similar ethical barometers: evil triumphs when the individual fails to exert control over his darkest impulses.

An analogous set of moral principles is at work in King's fiction as well. In *The Stand*, for example, those few remaining humans immune to the superflu are pulled between the two allegorical forces of good and evil, represented by Mother Abigail and Randall Flagg. Most of the characters who align themselves with Mother Abigail to establish a community in Colorado maintain their allegiance throughout, but *all* of these individuals—even the leaders of the group, Stu Redman and Nick Andros—are visited by Flagg, the latter appearing frequently in dreams of temptation, fear, and confusion. Only in actively confronting Flagg's influence do King's characters affirm the principle of goodness; Nadine Cross and Harold lauder, on the other hand, succumb to Flagg's machinations because they lack the self-discipline necessary to exert a moral will.

4

The discovery of evil is the central theme that writers in the American romance tradition share with King. The writers in this tradition have created characters who are a complex blend of good and evil, often committing their greatest sins in refusing to recognize the evil in themselves. This encounter with evil is frequently overwhelming; it does not always lead to a higher state of being. In fact its discovery often takes a violent shape—destructive of the central character or of others around him. Jack Torrance, Louis Creed, and Harold Lauder, like Benito Cereno, young Goodman Brown, and Poe's psychotic narrators in "William Wilson," "The Black Cat" and "The Cask of Amantillado," are not spiritually transformed by their discovery of the darker side of reality, but succumb to its horror and retreat into cynical pessimism.

On the other hand, the nineteenth century also supplies us with the possibility for spiritual regeneration within its strict moral precepts. Twain's Huckleberry Finn, Melville's Ishmael, and Hawthorne's Hester Prynne, Dimmesdale, Donatello, and Miriam, learn that there can be a certain strength derived from a descent into the abyss. King's protagonists suffer intensely to uncover a similar truth. His young heroes and heroines—Charlie McGee, Danny Torrance, Jack Sawyer, Mark Petrie, and those adults who are either affiliated with them or embody many of their attributes—inspire us with their efforts against despair and toward moral advancement. In this sense there exists a level of salvation available to King's characters that binds them to the "survivors" in the canons of Melville, Hawthorne, and Twain: the knowledge that moral maturity is a possible consequence from contact with sin. Their protagonists learn that they have within themselves the capacity for making ethical choices, and that these decisions will either enhance or retard their adjustment to the reality of evil. Once this awareness is established, the opportunity for a new and more confident personality emerges. It is the portrayal of this evolution that finally links King's fiction to the moral vision available in the nineteenth-century romance tradition—the ability to uplift his audience with the promise that painful insights into the horrors of our world can propel us beyond egotism or cynicism and toward the theory and practice of redemptive sympathy. Perhaps King's protagonists are unable to articulate it quite so adroitly, but they are nonetheless in a position to understand and share in the same spirit of transformation that informs Miriam's personality at the conclusion of Hawthorne's *The Marble Faun*: " '...sin—which man chose instead of good—has been so beneficently handled by omniscience and omnipotence, that, whereas our dark enemy sought to destroy us by it, it has really become an instrument most effective in the education of intellect and souls' " (840).

Chapter 2
"Crumbling Castles of Sand": The Social Landscape of King's Fiction

In the last decade America has witnessed the Stephen King phenomenon unfold in larger-than-life terms: his books can now be purchased in checkout lines of local grocery stories; his novels have been adapted into highly successful movies directed by artists as diversely talented as Stanley Kubrick, Brian De Palma, and Lewis Teague; his face and reputation promote American Express cards; and he is frequently interviewed in national magazines, tabloids, newspapers, journals, and on radio and television talkshows.

I have either heard or read at least a dozen of these interviews, and one of the first questions King is invariably asked is "why do you write horror fiction?" Typically, the author responds with the line "what makes you think I have a choice," and the discussion then descends into the arena of his fictional monsters and catastrophies and there it usually remains. To my knowledge, King has never been asked to define himself in any other terms; more specifically, in considering his work's relevance to real life in contemporary America. It is as if his interviewers take King at his literal word when he proclaims, as he does in the foreword to *Night Shift,* that his fiction "holds the reader or listener spellbound for a little while, lost in a world that never was, never could be" (xx). His newspaper and television interviews, perhaps because they are so short and must therefore focus on the most identifiable features of his canon, tend to reconfirm the popular view of Stephen King held by America's collective imagination: that his books are the literary equivalent to a roller coaster ride—composed primarily of fast thrills and chills and unexpected twists and turns.

In the foreword to *Night Shift*, King argues that the horror tale probes universal and primal phobias common to all human beings regardless of how, when, and where they live: "The great appeal of horror fiction through the ages is that it serves as a rehearsal for our own deaths" (xvi). For the individual reader the horror story is a symbolic reminder that the world is not always benevolently disposed to her welfare; indeed, it unlocks the latent fears that persist in the face of a good job, a good marriage, a healthy body. The horror genre raises existential issues that threaten our sense of well-being and complacency. Consequently, we repress them—sometimes even deny their possibility—and as a result, when we are presented with graphic illustrations of their reality, the effect is all the more unsettling.

It may be because the horror writer always brings bad news: you're going to die, he says; he's telling you to never mind Oral Roberts and his "something *good* is going to happen to you," because something *bad* is also going to happen to you, and it may be cancer and it may be a stroke, and it may be a car accident, but it's going to happen.... Those working in the genre with even the faintest understanding of what they are doing know that the entire field of horror and the supernatural is a kind of filter screen between the conscious and the subconscious; horror fiction is like a central subway system in the human psyche between the blue line of what we can safely internalize and the red line of what we need to get rid of in some way or another. (xxii)

King's more elaborative discourse in *Danse Macabre*, on the other hand, enlarges the scope beyond the personal to include a larger, cultural context for understanding the horror genre. The convoluted complexities of international economics, governmental bureaucracies, and the dramatic fluctuations in the status of world peace seem ever more beyond the individual's capacity for comprehension, much less within the realm of his influence. In *Danse Macabre*, King's explanation of the importance of the horror genre in film and literature is directly related to this sense of political and historical impotence; for King, a parallel exists between serious national economic or political stress and the emergence of books and films which portray (even symbolically) the cultural anxieties associated with such tensions:

...the horror genre has often been able to find national phobic pressure points, and those books and films which have been most successful almost always seem to play upon and express fears which exist across a wide spectrum of people. Such fears, which are often political, economic and psychological rather than supernatural, give the best work of horror a pleasing allegorical feel. . . . What scares us the most about Mr. Hyde, perhaps, is the fact that he was a part of Dr. Jekyll all along. And in an American society that has become more and more entranced by the cult of me-ism, it should not be surprising that the horror genre has turned more and more to trying to show us a reflection we won't like—our own. (18, 268)

Throughout *Danse Macabre*, King concentrates on providing a provocative social frame for appreciating the horror tale's relationship to modern American life. If these intimations on the horror genre likewise hold true for King's own fiction, and I submit that they do, his most persuasive tales are by necessity those which include the apparatus of the supernatural or speculative world in a direct confrontation with recognizable elements from the everyday or social realm. In his comprehensive and insightful essay on the origins of supernatural fiction "The Gothic Romance," Frederick S. Frank establishes several, frequently overlapping categories that define the major themes and tendencies of gothic literature. While Stephen King appears to have inherited the moral perspective Frank associates with the "High gothic" subheading, he also seems to belong in the category "Didactic or philosophical gothic." In defining this latter sub-grouping, Frank argues that the standard contraptions and supernatural phenomena of the gothic genre are "used to symbolize various political or religious concepts; the aim is to revolutionize or radicalize the thinking of the reader" (8). Although King would probably disclaim any allegiance with political revolution, his fiction is nonetheless politically focused—indeed, it is politically charged.

I believe that the tales of Stephen King are not merely excursions into a "world that never was, never could be," but that his best fiction, by contrast, is also a serious social fiction. The latter comprises a commentary on, and a critique of, modern America's value system—our politics, interpersonal relationships, our most revered and trusted institutions. His work describes a particular matrix in time; it bears a direct association with significant aspects of American culture and the types of human relationships it has engendered.

King's tales are filled with minute and accurate descriptions of American society: basketball hoops dot his two car suburban landscapes; we are told exactly what brand of cola or candy bar his characters ingest. But the writer's awareness of American life extends well beyond these superficial landmarks. He is also interested in probing some of our darkest and primal collective cultural fears: that the government we have installed through the democratic process is not only corrupt but actively pursuing our destruction, that our technologies have progressed to the point at which the individual has now become expendable, and that our fundamental social institutions—school, marriage, the workplace, and the church—have, beneath their veneers of respectability, evolved into perverse manifestations of narcissism, greed and violence. The particular horrors of King's novels are aligned with, and often emerge from, culturally specific disturbances; throughout his fiction there are signs that traditional concepts of social solidarity are fraying or have dissolved. Perhaps Harlan Ellison's inimitable writing style hyperbolizes the point, but his sense of the cultural crises at work in King's fiction is critically astute:

> Stephen King's books work as well as they do, because he is writing more of shadow than of substance. He drills into the flow of cerebro-spinal fluid with the dialectical function of a modern American mythos, dealing with archetypal images from the pre-conscious or conscious that presage crises in our culture even as they become realities. (77)

The stability of King's fictional universe is measured by moral choices: the men and women in his work struggle against the forces of evil, and from the encounter become less innocent. They are forced into decisions which make them better or worse, give their lives meaning or push them into despair. Many of his characters are not directly responsible for the situations in which they suddenly find themselves, but all of them must eventually respond to their particular circumstances—and they are judged accordingly. Indeed, the gothic machinery described so vividly in his novels and tales is more often than not revealed and/or aggravated by the failure of human love, immoral choices, and the dysfunction of cultural institutions and societal bonds.

The short story "Graveyard Shift" from the collection *Night Shift* is an apt illustration of King's use of horrific effects to underscore a breakdown in human communication. The tale takes place entirely in an old factory. The mill itself is an edifice that borrows heavily from the eighteenth-century gothic haunted castle, maintaining an internal life of its own: huge white toadstools and yellow mosses flourish in the basement, the building has a regulated "blood flow," while its gloomy floors, "lit only by the sputtering glow of fluorescents," (35) are the breeding grounds for an enormous rat population. But

"Graveyard Shift" is not merely a tale about an infested factory; there likewise exist important social implications as well.

Along with the rats, disgruntled human laborers inhabit the three upper levels of the mill. Throughout the narrative the reader sees repeated instances of man isolated from man: the mill workers mock and scorn one another, while Warwick, the shop foreman, shows a general disdain for the men working under him, continually taunting them for their laziness and stupidity. Even Hall, one of the young workers in the mill and the story's main character, is a man with neither roots nor purpose in life: "No wife, no steady girl, no alimony. He was a drifter...a solitary person" (35). The social interactions in this story show neither a sense of comradeship nor humanitarian vision. The level of alienation is highlighted by the fact that huge, physically deformed rats, some without back legs, others the size of cows, have established a thriving colony deep within the foundation of the factory itself: "Something happened to the rats back there. Some hideous mutation that never could have survived under the eye of the sun; nature would have forbidden it. But down here, nature had taken on another ghastly face" (49). The parallel is thus established between the human beings, who are treated like rats while working the night shift in this industrial haunted house, and the mutated rats themselves: both represent perversions of nature, unhappy and unhealthy defectives which owe their respective states of being to the factory itself.

The physical structure of the mill, each floor honeycombed with varying levels of rodent infestation, suggests the extent of worker-management stratification. Indeed, the men are virtually forced by management to confront the rats over a long (and ironically titled) Independence Day weekend. As Warwick warns his employees after one of them is savagely bitten by a huge rat: " 'This ain't no unionized shop, and never has been. Punch out now and you'll never punch back in. I'll see to it'" (43). The story's labor conflict reaches its nadir when Hall willingly sacrifices himself in order to obtain a modicum of "cold satisfaction" (48) in watching his foreman devoured by vermin. Near the end of the tale, Hall feeds Warwick to the swarming center of the rat colony, commenting sardonically, " 'the rats have business with you, I think'" (49). Only within the bowels of a subterranean landscape are manager and worker finally equal. Yet each man has been so warped by the perverse social nature of the workplace experience, that even their imminent deaths fail to exact the slightest degree of compassion:

They topped the miniature rise and looked down. Warwick reached it first, and Hall saw his face go white as paper. Spit ran down his chin, "Oh, my God. Dear Jesus."

And he turned to run.

Hall opened the nozzle of the hose and the high-pressure rush of water struck Warwick squarely on the chest, knocking him back out of sight. There was a long scream that rose over the sound of the water. Thrashing sounds....

"Goodbye, Warwick," Hall said. The rat crouched over Mr. Foreman jealously, ripping at one limp arm. (50)

"Graveyard Shift" is a succinct illustration of one of the writer's central moral maxims: when human beings fail to behave decently toward one another, they supply the opportunity for inhuman forces to manifest control. When the powers of science, religion and society cannot sustain meaningful and effective conceptions of human dignity and selfhood, the human world is immediately vulnerable to supernatural occurrences, and alienation and despair naturally follow. At the conclusion of "Graveyard Shift," the wooden trapdoor which preserved an imperfect barrier between the human and rodent communities is wrenched open, leaving the remaining factory workers vulnerable to the dominion of the rat.

1

Included in King's canon are multiple examples of marriages dissolving—"Strawberry Spring," "The Boogeyman," "Children of the Corn," "Word Processor of the Gods," *The Shining, Pet Sematary, Cujo, Thinner*—and in each of these instances marital discord and the undercurrent of divorce operate in some capacity to instigate or further exacerbate supernatural fury toward the human world. As I have mentioned already, King's representations of evil thrive on human weakness, so that when love is abandoned or unrequited, the human heart becomes receptive to cynicism and cruelty.

King's short tale "The Boogeyman" concerns a deeply disturbed man named Billings whose hostility toward the very concept of family reaches the point where he kills his own children. Although he is quick to blame their deaths on "the boogeyman," a creature who emerges from bedroom closets late at night, it is clear to the reader that the closet is a symbol for the repressed side of Billings' personality which is filled with resentment toward the responsibilities accompanying marriage.

Forced to leave college in order to find a job to support his new family, Billings reveals that he was torn between the love he felt for his wife and children and the desire to be free from the many difficult commitments this love entailed: "'Andy was an accident. That's what Rita said. She said sometimes that birth-control stuff doesn't work. I think that it was more than an accident. Children tie a man down, you know. Women like that, especially when the man is brighter than they.... It doesn't matter, though. I loved him anyway.' He said it almost vengefully, as if he had loved the child to spite his wife" (94).

Whether this narrative about the boogeyman-murderer is an extension of Billings' own warped psyche or an actual monster stalking him (as the conclusion might seem to suggest), is far less important that the creature's emergence coinciding with the breakdown of Billings' attitude toward family life. As such, the tale is a parallel to *The Shining*: unable to cope with the pressures and responsibilities of marriage, Jack Torrance and Billings lose control of themselves, drawing innocent wives and children into their respective psychotic nightmares.

In the short story "Children of the Corn," Vicky and Burt are sacrificed to the corn deity in large part because they have strayed from a commitment to marriage and to one another. Both appear as selfish, stubborn and unforgiving individuals. In fact, it is precisely because of their inability to communicate that Burt insists on remaining in Gatlin just long enough to discover the awful secret of the corn while drawing lethal attention to Vicky and himself: "Vicky was right. Something was terribly wrong here. He debated going back to Vicky without exploring any further, just getting into the car and leaving town as quickly as possible, never mind the Municipal Building. But it grated on him. Tell the truth, he thought. You want to give her Ban 5000 a workout before going back and admitting she was right to start with" (266).

In his provocative essay entitled "Cat and Dog: Lewis Teague's Stephen King Movies," Robin Wood asserts that King's books "insistently offer marriage and family as their major value, never seeming aware that there is any alternative" (39). As we have seen already in several examples, Wood's argument is well taken, but his line of reasoning might be extended to include a corollary: Those characters who stray from the intimate community of the nuclear family become immediately susceptible to evil. King seems to be implying that in the dissolution of marriage (or a love relationship), the cement which once bound individuals together in an acceptable social and psychological arrangement crumbles, and concurrent with this loss is a corresponding disintegration of self-discipline and moral purpose. Whenever they reject the internal security available in the familial arrangement, his characters are left vulnerable to the varied corruptions of the outside world. Once the traditional familial circle is broken, a parody of the marriage rite is performed between the male protagonist and an ambiguous and manipulative feminine force aligned with evil. In "Strawberry Spring," for example, Springheel Jack's urge to commit rape and murder is mysteriously fueled by a destructive, highly sexual feminine energy or principle contained within an early spring fog: "Springheel Jack was a man, no one seemed to doubt that, but the fog was his accomplice and it was female.... It was as if our little school was caught between them, squeezed in some crazy lover's embrace, part of a marriage that had been consumated in blood" (177).

Although technically not married to Frannie Goldsmith in *The Stand,* Harold Lauder's devotion is converted into acrimony when she rejects his affections for those of another man. His failed relationship with Frannie is the main impetus that leads Harold into the malevolent service of Randall Flagg, the novel's sinister clairvoyant and locus of evil. Harold's capacity for love, clearly in evidence throughout the first half of the novel in his loyalty to Frannie, is abandoned when he surrenders to Nadine Cross, Flagg's unholy version of Eve in this novel's desolate new world. Moreover, Nadine's seduction of Harold is not motivated by any kind of sincere passion, for she is only interested in the despoliation that occurs when Lauder's decadent fantasies are realized. After consummating these urges, Harold loses more than his virginity; his initiation into Nadine's dark sexuality deadens whatever ability he had to resist Flagg's moral corruption.

Images whirled giddily in his mind. Silk scarves...boots...leather-
...rubber. Oh Jesus. *Fantasies of a Schoolboy.* But it was all a kind of dream, wasn't it? A fantasy begotten of fantasy, child of a dark dream. He wanted all those things, wanted *her,* but he also wanted more.
    The question was, how much would he settle for?
    How long did he think? He didn't know. Later he wasn't even sure he had struggled with the question. But when he spoke the words tasted like death in his mouth: "In the bedroom. Let's go in the bedroom." (520-1)

The defilement of Harold Lauder effectively illuminates King's attitude toward sexual relationships when they become mere extensions of physical lust, devoid of love: King views this brand of sexuality as conducive to evil's design, perhaps even embodying it. If Lauder is a fiend, he is a sensitive fiend driven to fiendish acts out of pain, frustration, and misunderstanding. This is what happens when love is thwarted. Simple need may turn to evil. In this, Lauder's characterization is reminiscent of Jean Cocteau's film, "Beauty and the Beast," where, inscribed in Latin on the back of the Beast's chair, is the motto: "All men are beasts when they don't have love."

In *Cujo*, King's presentation of a rabid St. Bernard's slow disintegration from family pet to vicious fiend parallels the disintegration of the two families located at the center of the book. At night, young Tad Trenton is visited by a vague creature he is certain inhabits his closet. As the book unfolds, this monster reassembles in daylight—taking shape in Tad's mother's sexual infidelity, the consequent threat of his parents' divorce, and finally coalescing into the fury of Cujo's madness.

As Robin Wood argues convincingly, Cujo emerges as a great symbol of masculine aggression toward women that permeates the novel. His fury can be traced in Stephen Kemp, Donna Trenton's lover, who eventually unleashes his misogynistic anger on the entire Trenton household, Vic Trenton's own outrage when he discovers his wife's extramarital affair, and Joe Camber's abusive attitude toward his own wife and son. *Cujo* is King's most pessimistic book. Since its central theme is the essential inability of men and women to coexist harmoniously, Cujo's attack on Donna and Tad Trenton—a brutal two-day ordeal that is described in terms strongly resembling rape—represents a climax to the sexual tensions that characterize all of the book's impaired male-female interactions.

The breakdown of interpersonal relationships in both the workplace and the family is a recurring element in King's canon. The very real themes of marital discord, gender antagonism, and workplace alienation are avenues of access used by supernatural agents in their assault on the human realm. In spite of the imaginary landscapes which are often the settings for his tales and novels, King is profoundly aware of the discontents and conflicts which are exempla of contemporary American life. The horrific elements in King's world often emerge through the cracks of societal fragmentation, made visible and inescapable. These breakdowns are either directly responsible for unleashing the irrational forces of the underworld ("Graveyard Shift" and *The Shining*), or are indirectly reflected in the shape these forces assume (*Cujo* and *The Stand*).

2

The author's attitude toward the government—its bureaucratic system of controls and layers of deceit—is indicative of a post-Vietnam/Watergate skepticism engendered in many Americans of King's generation. The political backdrop for his fiction is summarized most concisely by the writer himself in this excerpt from *Danse Macabre*:

> Its [*The Stand's*] writing came during a troubled period for the world in general and America in particular; we had just witnessed the sorry end of the Nixon administration and the first presidential resignation in history, we had been resoundingly defeated in Southeast Asia, and we were grappling with domestic problems, from the troubling question of abortion-on-demand to an inflation rate that was beginning to spiral upward in a positively scary way.... These were changes enough to try and cope with, but on top of them, the America I had grown up in seemed to be crumbling beneath my feet...it began to seem like an elaborate castle of sand unfortunately built well below the high-tide line. (372)

King's personal reflections on the social influences which helped to shape *The Stand* are tantamount to casting a cultural context for his entire literary canon. The America described in his fiction knows defeat and sin; similar to the disillusionment the expatriates of Hemingway and Eliot's generation felt after World War I, King's characters always seem poised on the brink of new frontiers, left to struggle with a new set of cultural realities. The idealism of a mere decade earlier is suddenly inappropriate and will no longer suffice. Consequently, King's treatment of politics and the workings of governmental agencies in *The Stand*, *Firestarter*, and *The Dead Zone* continues to focus on the estrangement of individuals caught in the machinery of social institutions no longer adequate to contemporary needs. The American government is portrayed as divorced from the American people and operating without conscience. In King's novels, the same bureaucracy responsible for the misadventure of Vietnam has turned its vast resources and attention toward complicating and endangering the lives of private citizens. And just as we have traced the catastrophic results which occur when individuals stray from moral commitments to human fellowship, King's governmental representatives and political agents are either directly responsible for releasing the dual genies of science and the supernatural, or bear culpability for heightening already dangerous situations.

In *The Stand*, it is never made explicit who or what is liable for the superflu which devastates nearly the entire human population of the world. There is, however, a strong suggestion throughout the novel that the American government has played an instrumental role in the chemical experiments that initially unleashed the plague. As Deitz, an upper level government official, confesses to Stu Redman, " 'On this one the responsibility spreads in so many directions that it's invisible. It was an accident. It could have happened in any number of other ways'" (200). Until the flu actually destroys the government itself, its bureaucrats and scientists appear interested only in obfuscating blame for the plague's outbreak or tormenting those individuals like Stu Redman who possess an apparent immunity to the disease. The actual prospects of performing actions to ease suffering or honestly informing the country of its mistake are more foreign to the American government than the flu itself.

Similarly, in *The Mist*, it is a mistake that occurs at the "Arrowhead Project," a secret government installation engaged in specialized atomic research, that is responsible for the prehistoric creatures released to wreck havoc on the human population of a small Maine town (although the story implies that the mist may cover a much larger area). Just as the superflu in *The Stand* quickly moves beyond the reign of the American government and medical profession, leaving ordinary citizens to cope with an inconceivable disaster, in *The Mist* there are no bureaucratic or scientific representatives left to confront the consequences of their meddling and incompetence. In this novella, King's governmental portrait is as faceless—and unresponsive to human suffering—as the impalpable mist carrying its hidden reptilian peril.

If King's description of bureaucratic misconduct in *The Stand* and *The Mist* is measured in terms of a blundering but obscure force, in *Firestarter* these agencies of control assume a much more definite and ubiquitous form. Charlie McGee's childhood is abruptly and hideously fragmented by the government's unethical manipulation of her parents' chromosones and The Shop's desire to extend the experiment. As a result of the tinkering of biological phenomena neither understood nor respected, Charlie becomes the unwitting recipient of a genetic mutation that endows her with pyrokinetic abilities. As is often the case in King's fiction, her supernatural gift is in reality a curse; she must struggle to exert constant control over her every emotion so as to restrain this dangerous force that threatens everyone around her.

The greatest torment Charlie must undergo, however, is initiated by The Shop, a secret government organization comprised of sophisticated manipulators who not only murder both of Charlie's parents, but also engage in psychic blackmail in order to coerce her into refining her pyrokinetic talents for their own military purposes. As King reveals in a 1984 interview with Douglas Winter cited in the latter's book, *Stephen King: The Art of Darkness,*

The Shop is presented as a monolithic authority, but there is a very real sense that it is simply filled with bureaucrats who are running out of control. To me, the most horrifying scene in the book is the outright terrorism that goes on in a lunchroom when The Shop is looking for Andy and Charlie; this Shop agent terrorizes first a waitress and then a short-order cook—it's an awful piece of work. To suggest that there aren't guys like that who are actually getting their salaries from the taxpayers is to claim that there aren't guys like Gordon Liddy who ever worked for the CIA. And they love their work, man. They love their fucking work. (83)

Although he appears to operate outside the perimeters of all organized society, Rainbird, the psychotic Indian who believes that by murdering Charlie he will assume her powers in the afterworld, actually epitomizes the warped and unethical values that guide King's governmental agents, particularly those associated with The Shop. Both Rainbird and his employers seek to manipulate the girl's terrible powers to make themselves stronger. Unconcerned about Charlie's personal welfare except insofar as it furthers his own needs, Rainbird represents the purest evil in this novel of unscrupulous behavior; indeed, he possesses all the unsavory attributes of a Shakespearean villain: he is as arrogant as Edmund, as clever as Iago, as ruthless as Macbeth. In his role as Charlie's surrogate father, Rainbird maliciously exploits her confidence without conscience. Largely because of his callousness, Charlie must face her adolescence alone, left to contemplate an uncertain future of fear and flight. Even exposing her sordid tale to the news media is no guarantee that the government will abandon its quest to aggravate further the supernatural fury its own carelessness conceived.

King's perception of the federal government borders on paranoia. His men and women not only can expect to find no sanctuary from its agencies and officials, but have every reason to fear its tenacity and penchant for violence. As a result of their political disillusionment, the vast majority of protagonists in his novels and stories, like Johnny Smith in *The Dead Zone* and those survivors left to wander westward in *The Stand*, are bereft of sentimental attachments to patriotism. They are without faith in the traditional social institutions which managed to sustain Americans for generations.

The Dead Zone is not only a novel about the limitations inherent in the American political system, it also documents the ease with which unscrupulous aspirants to political office manipulate the momentum of a zealous following to increase their own attractiveness and strength. Greg Stillson is perhaps the most odious candidate to thunder through the pages of modern American fiction since Robert Penn Warren's characterization of Huey Long in *All the King's Men*. Stillson adheres to a similar value system as The Shop's: the single most important goal for both is the accumulation and preservation of power, and their energies remain dedicated to this principle. While The Shop operates beneath the cloak of secrecy, Greg Stillson hides behind a patriotic mask that disguises his ruthless ambition. Only Johnny Smith, in possession of a cognitive ability that permits him to glimpse the past and future whenever he touches an object or a person's hand, sees through Stillson's veneer to the nuclear holocaust he will initiate as president. The fact that Smith, through the aid of his hypersensitivity, is the only individual capable of separating the real Stillson from his deceptive personna, represents a clear indictment of an American electorate blindly supporting a political system that deliberately blurs the distinction between truth and illusion, the loud rhetoric of false patriotism and intellectual substance. There seems to be little doubt that King modelled Stillson after political demagogues such as Richard Nixon and Senator Joe McCarthy, two of the greatest—and most popular—masters of political sophistry in the modern era.

In his explicit detailing of Stillson's ascendency to power, King appears to be in tacit agreement with Alexis De Tocqueville's derisive warning in *Democracy in America* against the tendency toward collective misjudgment inherent in the American political system:

My greatest complaint against democratic government as organized in the United States is not, as many Europeans make out, its weakness, but rather its irresistible strength. What I find most repulsive in America is not the extreme freedom reigning there but the shortage of guarantees against tyranny. . . .

Hence the majority in the United States has immense actual power and a power of opinion which is almost as great. When once its mind is made up on any question, there are, so to say, no obstacles which can retard, much less halt, its progress and give it time to hear the wails of those it crushes as it passes.

The consequences of this state of affairs are fate-laden and dangerous for the future. (252, 248)

Like King, De Tocqueville fears the power of public opinion in America. In place of an aristocracy making absolute decisions that govern the behavior of others, American democracy puts this awesome responsibility into the hands of the majority, and this entity appears too easily swayed by the influence of emotionalism, the inability to distinguish subtle points of contradiction, a rabid need for conformity to its perspective, and a reluctancy to change its collective opinion. In King's treatment of these identical issues in *The Dead Zone*, the situation becomes more frightening than De Tocqueville could ever have imagined, as Stillson employs a media campaign that turns him into an instant celebrity. The fact that his political career is foiled by an accident of fate—a photographer captures him hiding behind a small child in an assassination attempt—indicates the vulnerability of the very system Greg Stillson comes close to controlling.

3

The criticism King directs toward his government and political institutions is not mollified in his depiction of organized religion. They are all characterized as spiritually bankrupt, functioning with neither a regard for life nor a concern for the consequences of illegal and illicit actions. Governmental and religious representatives dedicate themselves only to the perpetuation of authority and the methods necessary for maintaining it. And both carry out these methods with a calculating disregard for basic Christian principles. King's government lies perpetually to its citizens; religious authorities likewise deceive their congregations. As he explains in an interview with Douglas Winter in the collection *Faces of Fear*, the fictional portrayal of organized religion in his books is an untempered reflection of King's own personal beliefs: "It's very tough for me to believe in anything about organized religion. I think Jerry Falwell is a monster and I think Jimmy Swaggart is a monster" (242).

Contrary to the doctrines of his religious fundamentalists, in King's gothic landscape a Supreme Being either does not exist or has abandoned humankind to its own resources. In either case, as Carrie White discovers on the night of her prom, the choice between good and evil is a condition which belongs exclusively to the individual, and any attempt to relegate this responsibility to a higher being or religious dogma is subject to the writer's severest criticism: "She prayed and there was no answer. No one was there—or if there was, He/It was cowering from her. God had turned His face away.... And so she left the church, left it to go home and find her Momma and make the destruction complete" (200).

In *The Stand*, perhaps King's most religious book to date, the elaborate allegory embracing the ultimate conflict between the forces of good and evil in the world is eventually defined once again in distinctly human terms. At the novel's conclusion, Glen Bateman scorns Flagg's "regrettable lack of substance," because the devil's existence, like God's, is relegated to an abstraction; since Flagg's evil wears no human face, it is *less* than human and thus unworthy of Glen's fear: " 'You're *nothing*!' Glen said, wiping his streaming eyes and still chuckling. 'Oh pardon me...it's just that we were all so frightened...we made such a *business* out of you...' " (749).

Like *Carrie*, *The Stand* finally locates true religious sentiments within a secular context: the Free Zone endures because its citizens have not forgotten the importance of human love. Flagg's design to assassinate members of the Free Zone Committee can be carried out only after Nadine Cross relinquishes her own moral conscience (symbolized in her hair turning completely white) by ignoring "the voice that wouldn't stay dead, the voice that was now telling her to go back in there and pull the wires that ran between the blasting caps and the walkie-talkie" (575). Deciding to commit murder is a choice for which she is ultimately responsible; Flagg's domination of her life occurs only because she voluntarily elects to surrender it to him. Similarly, Stu Redman overcomes his life-threatening wounds and is reunited with Frannie not as a result of any divine intervention, but rather because a dog and a mentally retarded boy unselfishly administer to his physical needs and in the process rekindle Redman's own spirit of survival.

Glen Bateman's final written words, composed in a prison cell minutes before his death, tersely represent King's religious orientation as it appears throughout his canon: "I am not the potter, nor the potter's wheel, but the potter's clay; is not the value of the shape attained as dependent upon the intrinsic worth of the clay as upon the wheel and the Master's skill?" (748). If a divine Being does indeed coexist with humankind in animating King's world, Its influence is "dependent upon the intrinsic worth" of the men and women who give shape to Its destiny.

The religious dimension in King's work defies easy categorization. Like Hawthorne, he has been labeled a Puritan, an orthodox Christian, and a rational skeptic. Moreover, it is possible to consider both writers in all of these contexts, as there is some evidence to support each of these positions. As we have already seen, King and Hawthorne hold a number of ideas and attitudes in common, and Hawthorne's fiction comes closest to approximating King's vision of a religious faith. His respect for both the Puritan sense of moral earnestness and their acute understanding of human nature notwithstanding, Hawthorne's tales and novels, like those of King, suggest that redemptive grace is neither predetermined nor locked within the exclusive domain of a divine providence. Glen Bateman's personal insight into the mystery of man's relationship to God finds an echo in *The Scarlet Letter* and *The Marble Faun*. Both these books confirm that there exists no outward force capable of automatically saving a man through the dramatic power of divine intervention. The redemption made available to Dimmesdale, Miriam, and Donatello, is the product of a conscious and genuine change in the human heart. Hawthorne's men and women attain spiritual advancement only after their personal awareness of sin and guilt stimulates the actions of a heightened moral conscience. As in King, this progression is always humanly motivated and sustained; the changes necessary for this development are the results of conscious choices reflecting the free exercise of an enlightened human will. While the protagonists in King and Hawthorne frequently find themselves in circumstances they do not fully comprehend and exposed to forces over which they can not exert full control, their choice of behavior within the context of these circumstances dictates whether or not they will grow in self-awareness or succumb to self-destruction. Thus, there are tragedies throughout the fictions of Hawthorne and King, but there is also the potential for heroic action so long as characters refuse to surrender themselves to despair. As Bernadette Bosky proposes in "The Mind's a Monkey: Character and Psychology in Stephen King's Recent Fiction," "even in the face of overpowering evil something good and positive in the human spirit will be saved" (213).

The religious zealots in King's fiction, like the social reformers in Hawthorne's, deny "what is good and positive in the human spirit" because they refuse to accept the reality of a free will. His religious extremists have abandoned man—the complexities and contradictions of his soul—to a mechanistic design that takes the responsibility for existence out of the individual's control. They are thereby able to rationalize even their most odious actions because they perform them under the belief that they are serving God's Will. The children in "Children of the Corn," Sunlight Gardner in *The Talisman*, Mrs. Carmody in *The Mist*, Johnny Smith's mother in *The Dead Zone*, and Margaret White in *Carrie*, all worship an Old Testament Jehovah and maintain at least a verbal commitment to Christ as personal savior. Beneath their veneer of piety, however, is a vicious credo of depravity and insanity. What makes their sophistries so reprehensible is that they often ensnare unsuspecting children, forever warping them from the pursuit of normal lives. In destroying these children, their behavior serves as an ironic commentary on the Old Testament promise that "the sins of the father shall be visited on the young."

Sunlight Gardner, for example, is as adept at administering sadistic punishments as he is in quoting scripture. Although he pretends to serve Christ's ministry at the Sunlight Home for wayward boys, he is in reality one of Morgan Sloat's most brutal henchmen. Similarly, Carrie's fundamentalist upbringing so ingrains the spirit of violence inherent in Christianity into her personality—Christ's blood sacrifice, the money changers beaten in the temple, the Last Judgment—that her entire attitude toward the world is shaped within this limited context. The various humiliations she suffers as an outsider at Ewen High School conform perfectly with her mother's religious pronouncements that life consists only of pain and negation. And since Margaret White has inadequately prepared her daughter with the adjustment skills necessary for survival in the real world (she translates Carrie's menstrual period into a symbol of corruption sent by God to punish women), Carrie's telekinetic rage becomes a grotesque reflection of her own religious indoctrination and personal experience. The young woman's frustrations build to the point at which she simply capitulates to her mother's vision of the world: "Carrie sat with her eyes closed and felt the black bulge of terror rising in her mind. Momma had been right, after all. They had taken her again, gulled her again, made her the butt again. The horror of it should have been monotonous, but it was not" (182). Religious extremism fills Carrie with such a degree of self-loathing and disgust that normal development becomes impossible. Just as the American government both engendered and refined Charlie McGee's destructive capabilities in *Firestarter*, the perverse influence of religious fanaticism propels Carrie toward her night of carnage.

4

The real horrors in Stephen King's canon are sociopolitical in nature. His work documents the contemporary strain on American social institutions. The surreal and fantastic occurrences which take place throughout his canon are, as we have seen, often symbolic representations of a larger cultural crisis. Grotesque and furious manifestations of misanthropic forces fill the void created by the absence of meaningful interpersonal relationships, responsible and responsive government, and a supportive system of benevolent religious faith.

The collapse of American cultural and societal traditions leaves many of King's characters confronting spiritual and physical crises, beset with the need to uncover solutions to the malaise of a dead or dying world. The last two chapters of this book consider the options Stephen King provides his characters to aid in their quest to restructure social relationships and to affirm a new moral vision; these last chapters offer alternatives to the social waste land King affiliates with contemporary America. Before turning in this direction, however, we must first examine the other features of King's fiction which are likewise responsible for weakening the barriers separating the human world from the bestial.

Chapter 3
Motorized Monsters:
The Betrayal of Technology

In Stephen King's early short story "Trucks," a small group of men and women huddle in a diner that is under siege from a caravan of driverless buses and trucks. While these machines restlessly patrol the parking lot surrounding the restaurant searching for more humans to attack, a former truck driver inside the building stares out the window in disbelief. Although he is obviously confused about the irrational events taking place in front of him, his reaction is less anger or fear than a sense of deep disappointment—as if his rig has somehow betrayed him personally: "'I ain't had no problems with my rig. She's a good old girl.... Been driving her for six years' " (130).

While King offers no definitive explanations as to why the trucks have, like Hitchcock's birds, suddenly turned against the human world, the implication is that the machines' masters have violated nature's order, and in doing so have managed to disrupt a mysterious equilibrium, leaving the modern world suddenly juxtaposed with a prehistoric one:

> We could run, maybe. It would be easy to make the drainage ditch now, the way they're stacked up. Run through the fields, through the marshy places where trucks would bog down like mastodons and go— *back to the caves.*
>
> Drawing pictures in charcoal. This is the moon god. This is a tree. This is a Mack Semi overwhelming a hunter. (142)

Throughout the story King makes reference to prehistoric time, suggesting that although we trust in the evolution of civilization, these advances have and will continue to betray us, so that the perceived distance that comfortably separates modern man from his prehistoric ancestor may not be nearly as great as we might like to believe.

The world-view of "Trucks" is repeated continually in King's fictional descriptions of modern technology. The human world produces mechanical devices to aid it, but these machines usually fail to perform in the manner for which they were created. In this particular tale, the diner's counterman urges his fellow humans to refuse the trucks' request for fuel, " 'Stay in here,' he said. 'You want to spend the rest of your life changin' oil filters every time one of those...*things* blasts its horn?' " (137). Ironically, what the counterman does not comprehend is that in King's fiction the American landscape is filled with examples of men who have already become slaves to the technologies they have invented. Consequently, each time the machine age is represented in his work, it is inevitably cast in a negative context, as antagonistic to human welfare and values. And correspondingly, those individuals who align themselves with the spirit of the technological age most often do so at the expense of their humanity, becoming mere appendages of the machines themselves.

1

In *Of a Fire on the Moon*, Norman Mailer describes America's space program as the "quintessential statement of our fundamental insanity" (217). In their need to conquer and their pride in themselves and their technology, Mailer believes our astronauts may well be in violation of the divine order of the universe. For Mailer this urge to extend our dominion and power beyond the earth is man's most hubristic act. The ascent in the same kind of machinery that has made the earth a potential catastrophe is the ultimate desecration of the natural order.

The character of Randall Flagg in *The Stand* is a descendant of the perverse technological legacy Mailer examines in *Of a Fire on the Moon*. Glen Bateman describes Flagg as a natural consequence and extension of the technological god that was worshipped prior to the plague: " 'Maybe he's just the last magician of rational thought, gathering the tools of technology against us' " (474). As such, his role in this book provides another illustration of King's jaundiced perspective on modern America— a society that has sacrificed its moral integrity to the quest for synthetic productivity.

Although Flagg's evil is affiliated throughout the novel with forces as diverse and ubiquitous as Satan and the wild creatures of the night, he is best represented in technological terms. His vision of the future is conceivable only by resurrecting the tools of the past. In order to help him to attract and maintain the allegiances of the Las Vegas denizens, one of Flagg's first priorities as emperor of this desert city is to insure that the energy and communication conduits are re-opened, essentially returning Vegas to its pre-plague reality. And while we are told of his success at reconnecting air conditioning generators and telephones, his ultimate goal is to reactivate the technologies of war, once more summoning the same lethal powers that were responsible for producing the plague in order to fulfill his fantasy of worldly conquest. In one of his dreams Flagg envisions himself preparing for battle against the Free Zone, but the dark man does not interpret himself as a military strategist whose consumate skills as a commander make victory possible. Instead, his identification is with the raw power afforded by controlling the leftover hardware of a nation that was obsessed with its various engines of destruction:

> In the dream he saw an army of ten thousand raggle-taggle castoff men and women driving east, a rough beast of an army whose time had come round at last, loading down trucks and jeeps and Wagoneers and campers and tanks;... And riding in their van atop a giant tanker with pillow tires, he saw himself, and knew that the truck was filled with jellied napalm...and behind him, in column, were trucks loaded with pressure bombs and Teller mines and plastic explosives; flame throwers and flares and heat-seeking missiles; grenades and machine guns and rocket launchers. (368)

The amorphous qualities of Randall Flagg are suggested early in the novel. In his pockets are tracts that represent the extremities of political thought—from pamphlets advocating Blacks for Militant Equality to the Kode of the Klan (119). It is appropriate that he holds to no ideological commitment; for Flagg, like technology itself, ultimately subsists outside the realm of human politics. He adroitly manipulates the radical fringes— those groups on both the political left and right who suffer the most frustration, fear, and anger—to aid in his goal of spreading chaos and hatred: "He had helped lay plans that resulted in the kidnapping of an heiress, and it had been he who suggested that the heiress be made crazy instead of ransomed. He had left the small Los Angeles house where De Freeze and the others had fried not twenty minutes before the police had arrived" (122).

At the core of Flagg's deliberate, albeit contradictory, personality, then, we find the same impulses toward self-destruction and betrayal that characterize King's portrait of

modern technology. Flagg embodies the two opposing forces of
anarchy and fascism. He seeks to foment political chaos within
the world, yet under his tyrannical leadership Las Vegas is
transformed into "an atmosphere of tight discipline and linear
goals" (396). The history of modern technology affords us a
similar set of paradoxes: the splitting of the atom resulted in
both the threat of nuclear annihilation and the production of
alternative energy; biomedical research has spawned the
unnatural twins of germ warfare and artificial insemination.
These two sides of technology appear indivisible, and it is within
King's province as a writer of modern horror fiction to remind
us that every scientific advancement brings it attendant anxieties.

Because Trashcan Man echoes Flagg's tendency toward
psychopathic behavior as well as his fascination with the potential
destruction available in America's discarded technologies of war,
it is not surprising that the two men gravitate toward one another.
Trashcan Man is the dark man's technological "id"; he mirrors
Flagg's madness and self-destructive impulses, while possessing
none of his tyrannical self-discipline.

> His skin had burned, peeled, burned, peeled again, and finally it had
> not tanned but blackened. He was walking proof that a man finally takes
> on the look of what he is. Trash looked as if someone had doused him
> in #2 kerosene and struck a match to him. The blue of his eyes had faded
> in the constant desert glare, and looking into them was like looking into
> weird, extra-dimensional holes in space. He was dressed in a strange imitation
> of the dark man—an open-throated red-checked shirt, faded jeans, and desert
> boots that were already scratched and mashed and folded and sprung. (704)

Trash is a technological genius—he knows how to
manipulate the deadly machinery that is all around him—but
he can create nothing, he can only destroy. In this sense he is
emblematic of "blind science"; his personal madness is
symptomatic of the greater insanity which has led to the
construction and deployment of America's lethal gadgetry. Under
their design to employ civilization's final and most sophisticated
legacy—the nuclear bomb—Flagg and Trashcan Man ironically
reveal their link to the barbarism of primitive man, with none
of the latter's humility in the face of powers greater than the
self. The reader's most visual sense of Trashcan Man is reflected
in the above description: a human scorpion wandering through
the Nevada desert, suffering from an advanced stage of radiation
sickness, parched and severely sunburned. His physical and
mental scars are meant to suggest the same spiritual desolation

that is at the heart of T.S. Eliot's critique of modern man in *The Waste Land:*

> Son of man,
> You cannot say, or guess, for you know only
> A heap of broken images, where the sun beats,
> And the dead tree gives no shelter, the cricket no relief,
> And the dry stone no sound of water. (I, 20-24)

In the void of love for someone or something other than themselves, Flagg and Trashcan Man serve only the "broken images" of technology—the dark religion of destruction that merely reflects, like the heat from one of Trashcan's oil conflagrations, their own self-loathing: "More and more [Flagg] felt an urge to simply act, to move, to do. To destroy" (698). It is therefore significant that Trash eventually betrays his master, turning his technological expertise against the black man by first destroying his aircraft and eventually his entire kingdom. The apocalypse he helps to produce under the misapprehended belief that he is making reparation to Flagg merely underscores the essential distrust and inevitable potential for self-annihilation that King associates with any attempt to harness the powers of technology: "He had thought Trashcan Man could be thrown away like a defective tool. But he had succeeded in doing what the entire Free Zone could not have done. He had thrown dirt into the foolproof machinery of the dark man's conquest" (699).

If Flagg and his Las Vegas empire are both reflective of, and destroyed by, the betrayal of technology, the Free Zone survives because its inhabitants initially refuse to sacrifice themselves to recreating another version of the pre-plague world. Although their lifestyle is rudimentary in comparison to the comforts available in Las Vegas, the Boulder community unconsciously revels in the distinctions that separate it from modern western societies:

> Men and women were living together with no apparent desire to reinstitute the ceremony of marriage. Whole groups of people were living together in small subcommunities like communes. There wasn't much fighting. People seemed to be getting along. And strangest of all, none of them seemed to be questioning the profound theological implications of the dreams...and the plague itself. Boulder itself was a cloned society, a *tabula so rasa* that it could not sense its own novel beauty. (427)

Moreover, while the citizens of Las Vegas (especially those with technocratic backgrounds) are attracted to Flagg because he is the wizard of technology, the members of the Free Zone cling to Mother Abagail's primitive mysticism and simple faith in God. Her "white magic" is decidedly anti-technological in its orientation; when she seeks greater power to aid her in guiding the community, she follows the examples of biblical prophets and religious mystics by wandering into the woods to seek correspondence with the unharnessed and inhuman powers of the natural world. The four Free Zone men who initiate the collapse of Flagg's dominion do so by following Mother Abagail's instruction and example: shunning automobiles, weapons, and the other machinery of modern America, they journey to the heart of Flagg's empire relying only upon their instincts and courage. The fact that these attributes are sufficient to overpower Flagg's superior forces suggests the inevitable fate awaiting all those who sacrifice moral responsibility in favor of a commitment to technology. The precise fears that King dramatizes in *The Stand* are perhaps most accurately summarized by Douglas Winter in *The Art of Darkness:*

We pursue happiness, believe in progress, materialism, and the infallibility of science, but we doubt our success, our power, ourselves. As we watch the evening news, if we reflect even momentarily upon our social fabric, we begin to question the validity of the engine of progress. Our position as a society is a precarious one—and principally because of our misguided belief in the divinity of civilization and technology. (58)

King's 1983 novel *Christine* is best understood in light of the many examples of technological betrayal which can be traced throughout his fiction. Christine is representative of a myth and an era. The American automobile—especially in the 1950s—was a great mirror for America itself. It reflected the era's cheap gas, a nearly completed interstate highway system, the country's economic prosperity, and most important, an infatuation with the new frontiers of speed and space. Moreover, in the late 1950s the machine age was no longer an avoidable facet of existence; Americans had little choice but to adapt to the pace of the machine, as the engines of technology became as important as the individual lives who created and serviced them. This scientific advance, as Thomas Hine points out in his book *Populuxe*, was viewed as a necessary, if sometimes dehumanizing, development in the course of American progress. "The Bomb's brilliant glow," claimed a housewife's testimonial in a 1954 ad, "reminds me of the brilliant gleam Beacon Wax gives to floors."

2

Christine takes the denouement of "Trucks" to its logical extreme: this 1958 Plymouth Fury is the ultimate in technological mastery; human beings prove superfluous to its existence as the automobile is capable of fixing itself. Equally as significant, the ability to regenerate itself is born from a bond between machine and malefic forces. As is pointed out on several occasions throughout the book, Christine "has the devil riding shotgun" (365). The nexus between machinery and evil appears elsewhere in King's fiction—"Trucks," "The Mangler," "Lawnmower Man," "Sometimes They Come Back," "The Monkey" and the boiler in *The Shining* are memorable examples. In these tales, as well as in *Christine*, the rational philosophy that gave birth to the machine age has been systematically displaced by irrational and malevolent forces. As we found in King's descriptions of America's social institutions discussed in the preceding chapter, these same forces often animate King's supernatural phenomena, and usually emerge as a direct consequence of human transgression. King's "technological monsters" would seem to suggest a similar breakdown in the association between human and nonhuman worlds. The order governing this relationship has become perverted so that the humans, who have grown increasingly dependent on this faceless technology, find themselves no longer in control of it. Indeed, in our quest to free ourselves by inventing the technologies of work and leisure, we literally have had to free the machine. And as we have traced in Chapter 2, when the mortal world abdicates responsibility for its actions and creations, a conduit is opened allowing supernatural demons to manifest dominion. At one point in *Christine*, George Le Bay argues that the evolution of science has always occurred "outside humanity." But the implications of his reasoning, to which Le Bay remains blissfully naive, suggest that many of the consequences of these advancements are also adverse to humanity's well-being:

"Comes the Civil War and all at once it's 'ironclad time.' Then it's 'machine-gun time.' Next thing you know it's 'electricity time' and 'wireless time' and finally it's 'atom-bomb time.' As if those ideas all come not from individuals but from some great wave of intelligence that always keeps flowing...some wave of intelligence that is outside of humanity." (105)

Through his involvement with Christine, Arnie initially participates in the freedom that has always represented the most attractive aspect of technology: he asserts his independence from his parents as well as the high school boys who have intimidated him, he comes of age romantically and sexually, he even rids himself of acne. Ironically, Arnie's freedom, and this again is meant to symbolize King's perspective on the price of human emancipation when it is purchased through technological implementation, is actually a form of entrapment. Like Jack Torrance's relationship with the machinery of the Overlook hotel, Arnie is fatally attracted to the promise of power and success which always appears to be just beyond his reach, resting securely in the confident hands of a Dennis Guilder or someone else. Inside his motorized "dream machine," however, the promise is made flesh:

> It seemed to him that there were things Leigh could not understand, things she could never understand. Because she hadn't been around. The pimples. The cries of *Hey Pizza-Face!* The wanting to speak, the wanting to reach out to other people, and the inability. The impotence. It seemed to him that she couldn't understand the simple fact that, had it not been for Christine, he never would have had the courage to call her on the phone even if she had gone around with I WANT TO DATE ARNIE CUNNINGHAM tattooed on her forehead. (199-200)

Arnie pays for the above transformation, on the other hand, in the loss of his best friend, in severing all contact with his family, and in forfeiting his only opportunity to experience mature love with a woman. Christine is a jealous mistress. Through her mysterious association with Roland Le Bay, the automobile succeeds in converting Arnie into her slave. Consequently, a terrible price is exacted (both in sacrificing his identity as well as his life) for Arnie's involvement with the freedom of the machine.

3

While it is apparent that Arnie has been chosen by Christine, or perhaps Le Bay, to be the one to resurrect the automobile, it is also true that he has likewise chosen her. Like Victor Frankenstein in Mary Shelley's novel, Arnie is obsessed with providing life to an inanimate object: "'She could be fixed up. She could be tough. A moving unit, Dennis. A beauty...there's something underneath. Something else.... I don't think she's any ordinary car' " (29-30). As Arnie and Victor Frankenstein grow ever more involved with their artificial creations, both men undergo their own physical and psychological changes. Each time Frankenstein sees the monster, he falls into a deep fever; this illness is the visible manifestation of his own guilt for the murders his creation has commissioned. While Arnie initially experiences his own personal renaissance, he deteriorates rapidly once Christine begins her rampage of revenge against Repperton and his gang. From the beginning of his work on the monster, Frankenstein's obsession likewise causes him to lose contact with his family and friends: "The same feelings which made me neglect the scenes around me caused me also to forget those friends who were so many miles absent, and whom I had not seen for a long time. I know my silence disquieted them" (55). Moreover, once the scientist rejects his creation, the monster begins to murder all of the people close to Victor: his younger brother, best friend, and finally his wife on their wedding night. Like Victor, Arnie Cunningham grows ever more isolated from those around him, making choices that ultimately destroy whatever ties he shared with his family and friends. These choices include deciding that Christine is the most important element in his life. Leigh Cabot tells him " 'if you really loved me, you'll get rid of it,' " but faced with this ultimatum, Arnie chooses Christine: " 'I don't need you! I don't need any of you!' " (322).

In a scene easily overlooked, Dennis' father recounts a brief episode from his past. As a young man he made the choice to refuse employment as Darnell's tax accountant. Since Guilder understood that Darnell's illegal business dealings would require him to make severe moral compromises, " 'I made it clear pretty early on that I didn't want to dance' " (115). The role Dennis' father plays elsewhere in this book is really quite insignificant; it is as if King placed him in the narrative for the expressed purpose of this single episode. In his conversation with Dennis he illustrates the moral decisions each of us must make in life. His choice to reject Darnell's offer of employment serves as a deliberate contrast with Arnie's willingness to sacrifice himself and those around him for the "promises" Christine is capable of granting. Out of his fear for Cunningham, Guilder warns his son that " 'good people can sometimes get blinded, and it's not always their fault' " (116), but the example of his own life's choices would appear to suggest that the human will is free enough and strong enough to avoid such predicaments.

As their obsessions with machinery deepen, Victor Frankenstein and Arnie Cunningham lose control over their lives, relinquish relationships which were formerly important, and experience tragic deaths. Neither has been able to destroy the creation they have let loose on the world. And they both die having failed to free themselves from their mistakes. Dennis may feel that "Arnie fought him [Le Bay]—and earned at least a draw" (493), but the sobering conclusion of the novel, implying that Christine may return for yet another round of terror, indicates otherwise.

The moral lessons of *Frankenstein* and *Christine* tell us that as man becomes more reliant on his technological creations, he comes to resemble them in his insensitivity and moral impotence. Moreover, an implicit warning exists in both books that has received recent confirmation in the mistakes which occurred at Three Mile Island, Love Canal, and the Rhine River: the more sophisticated our technological expertise, the greater the potential of our losing control over it. And should this occur, as Arnie and Victor illustrate, we stand in jeopardy of losing ourselves.

4

In his introduction to the edited collection *Science-Fiction: The Future*, Dick Allen draws some valuable distinctions among texts in the genre. The more pessimistic side of science-fiction, he argues, "stresses the dangers of the machine age and how reliance upon science and technology weakens the basic human body and spirit" (7). This awareness of the darker aspects of technology and the moral sacrifices that accompany its proliferation is an issue that often appears in King's fiction. I have heard King deliver several public lectures in the past few years and in each instance he has made some sort of reference to his omnipresent fear of nuclear war. In his November 6, 1986 address as the Elliott Lecturer at the University of Maine, Orono, for example, King told his audience that he has paid enough tax money to the federal government so that "somewhere under the cornfields of Kansas there is now a Titan missile with *'Salem's Lot* written on its side." A primary impetus that led to King's support of Gary Hart's presidential campaign in 1984 was his belief that among all the political aspirants to this office, Hart provided the best assurance that "my missile will remain in its silo." In *The Stand* Glen Bateman articulates a similar worry when he speculates that "if Communities A and B both have pet technicians, they might work up some kind of rusty nuclear exchange over religion, or territoriality or some paltry ideological difference" (227).

In his fictional portrayals of America's technologies— nuclear and otherwise—King seeks to scare his readership into contemplating the consequences of the "gadgets" this society is producing. As he explained to Douglas Winter in an interview published in *Faces of Fear*,

> So now we have nuclear bombs, we have stuff that can kill twenty million people in twelve seconds. CBW, nerve gas, the nukes, all this stuff, it's just gadgets, that's all it is. Our technology has outraced our morality. And I don't think its possible to stick the devil back in the box. I think that it will kill us all in the next twenty years.
>
> ...Even if we don't go on, if you've got twelve minutes before the missiles land, you turn around and the kid says to you, "I understand the world is ending, Dad. What did you do to stop this from happening?" And you say, "Well, I played my Doors tapes." It doesn't work. "I gave to CARE. When the UNICEF volunteer came to my door, I gave what I could." You can't say that, it's not sufficient. (253)

In King's hands, the technohorror story illustrates the impotence of science in the face of the monumental problems it is directly responsible for creating. The writer poses some unsettling answers to the distinctly modern question of whether man, the great destroyer of the natural world, is of nature or above her. The technology we employ to overcome nature also separates us from it. His novels and tales often link governmental bureaucracies and science in an unholy tryst: both tinker blindly and immorally with aspects of nature they neither respect nor comprehend. There are no golden futures in King's portrait of contemporary technology, no scientists who come to save a beleagured humanity, as was the case in much of the science fiction that was written during its halcyon years in the 1950s. The newspapers written in the two decades since have exposed too many flaws in the crystal palace of science. As a consequence, King wishes to impress upon us the importance of taking responsibility for the decisions made by our society. Like Hawthorne a century earlier, King warns us against seeking perfection and getting involved in areas beyond our comprehension, since we, as humans, are imperfect. He shows us, moreover, that when we seek to harness the mysteries of nature—to imitate God—we leave ourselves open to the forces of chaos. A natural world stripped of its mysteries, either through technology or self-conceit, only reinforces our sense of being alone in the universe, our fear of mortality, our feelings of insignificance. Most of all, like Stu and Franny at the conclusion of *The Stand*, King's fiction resonates with a plea to teach our children to avoid the mistakes of their elders.

Chapter 4
"Barriers Not Meant to be Broken": Dark Journeys of the Soul

In recent years much has been written about Stephen King's unique brand of horror. The manner in which he actually achieves these horrific effects, however, still remains only vaguely defined in the emerging corpus of King criticism: are there identifiable patterns to the shape horror takes in his fiction, and more specifically, when do these elements emerge and how are they most often released?

Some readers may well question the importance of examining these issues at all; isn't it enough that King's work is enjoyable to read? Why bother complicating it? Don Herron supports just such an anti-interpretive stance in his essay "The Biggest Horror Fan of All," arguing that there can be no valid accounting for King's supernatural events, and any attempt to analyze the reasons for their occurrences takes all the fun out of being scared by them. Besides failing to apprehend the orientation that informs the greater part of King's treatise on the symbolic representations of horror presented in *Danse Macabre*, Herron's anti-intellectual insistence that we avoid "explaining the deeper meaning of going into a horror fun house" (39) ultimately does a disservice to King's canon as well as to other serious contributions to the genre. King, like Hitchcock before him, is providing an implicit critique of ourselves and American culture as he simultaneously titillates us with grotesque chimera; at their very best (or, worst) both Hitchcock and King blend the modern tale of horror into the painful mystery of authentic tragedy. In Hitchcock's *Psycho*, for example, the crime of robbery and subsequent violation of personal conscience are the events which precipitate the young secretary's grisly death in the infamous shower scene; similarly, middle-class American values and courtship rituals are subtly criticized as potential causes for the sudden ecological upheaval that occurs in *The Birds*. Both Hitchcock and King are artists in possession of acute moral insight, and the horror elements in their work cannot be separated from this vision.

In his justification why the horror film deserves serious critical attention, Frank Manchel reminds us that "any art form that has such a massive audience deserves study. From each study we can perhaps learn something about ourselves and our society" (8). Art and artists do not work in cultural vacuums; to greater or lesser degrees, it is quite impossible to separate the artistic vision (or whatever inspiration is responsible for it) from the exact historical time and place in which it occurs. Herron's demand that horror fiction remain exempt from the confluential and interpretive scholarship long associated with mainstream literature, effectively reduces the importance and quality of horror fiction as art; it erroneously presupposes that horror fiction is somehow composed differently from other art, and for too long this false dichotomy has helped to relegate the horror genre to an inferior status—distinct from, and subordinate to, "classical" literature.

1

One of the more distinguishing features that links King's work to its historical time and place is the readily recognizable commercial brand names of contemporary America. Because many of these references initially appear to be nothing more than innocuous aspects of American life, they often lull the reader into a false sense of security so that the terror, when sprung, becomes all the more terrifying. In an interview with Douglas Winter cited in *The Art of Darkness*, Burton Hatlen, one of King's most influential English teachers, points out that his former pupil discovered "there was not an absolute, unbridgeable gulf between the academic culture and popular culture, and that he could move back and forth between the two...it enabled him to become what he wanted to be—a serious writer in American literature as well as a best seller" (22).

King's landscapes are littered with the well-known brand names of corporate America for several reasons. First, he seeks to reproduce a detailed and highly visual sense of the real world— in order to subvert it. If the reader can be convinced that King's characters are actually functioning in our world, that they ingest the same foods, drive upon the same interstate highways, listen to the same rock lyrics, then the horror they experience becomes ours; and certainly that horror must become all the more plausible and frightening as a result of this personal identification. As Ben Indick has observed in his essay "King and the Literary Tradition of Horror," "King has put [terror] into the shopping basket, next to the tomato sauce, the Sanka and the Tab. Fear has become a commonplace, no longer the evil dispensation of noble or supernatural forces" (188). Secondly, King pursues the values of commercial America to their illogical extreme: in a society where material objects are often treated with more dignity than the people who use them, it is only slightly ironic that many of these goods frequently attain a "life of their own." Indeed, a 1958 Plymouth Fury and a luxury hotel in Colorado are restive because of the human misconduct which has occurred within them over the years. In both these cases it is apparent the evil in the inanimate object pre-existed the current identifier, yet gained much of its strength from human sources. Similarly, the town of Las Vegas, that magnificent symbol of American decadence and greed, becomes the locus for Randall Flagg's legions of evil. These correlations are not accidental, and they are important because they reveal a crucial nexus between overwhelming evidence of reprehensible human behavior and the release of supernatural phenomena beyond mortal control.

Instances of moral transgressions that are either directly or indirectly responsible for triggering terrifying antihuman responses are repeated continually throughout King's canon: when humanity behaves immorally, an extrahuman force emerges to render devastation. Elsewhere in this book we have examined the textual evidence supporting this thesis within a technological and sociocultural context. In novels as diverse as *Firestarter, The Stand, The Dead Zone, The Mist* and *The Talisman,* King's warning is explicit: individuals sacrifice themselves and their loved ones to psychological trauma and potential annihilation whenever any institutional organization is put into a position to influence their lives.

2

The appearance of horrific effects and violent supernatural occurrences in King's fiction, however, is not exclusively limited to the domains of American political, cultural, and technological liabilities. Beneath the deepest levels of governmental and social corruption in King's books is a force even darker and more frightening: the ineradicable corruption of the human heart. The dissolution of personal moral codes, then, is another instance of terror being allowed to reign in King's fictional microcosm.

The weakening of ethical codes of conduct—whether occurring on the societal or individual plane—sets off some form of retribution in the emergence of vehement supernatural energies.

Perhaps this Old Testament world-view is partially the result of King's own fundamentalist background as a child, although if this is indeed the case it is the only element of a fundamentalist tradition King appears to have inherited. His faceless gods are neither just nor discriminating in their punishments. In his novels, the degree of retribution that attends human transgressions is always punitive and apparently ceaseless; moreover, once the creatures of the underworld are unleashed, their wrath often encompasses everyone within range, even those innocent of the cause of their emergence. As Douglas Winter has pointed out, King's "version of God harkens less to modern Christian values and their source, the New Testament, than to those of the Old Testament, and particularly the Book of Job" (127).

In the short story "Uncle Otto's Truck," an abandoned Cresswell pick-up truck, rotting quietly in a meadow, is spontaneously regenerated after it is used by Otto as a murder weapon to eliminate his partner, McCutcheon. Although Otto's nephew, the young narrator of the tale, initially dismisses his uncle's claim that the machine " 'gets a little bit closer every year' " (388) as the paranoid delusions of a guilty conscience, the story's conclusion appears to support the probability that Otto's crime has somehow activated a revenging principle within the truck itself. The narrator is a witness to his uncle's demise:

> When I first saw the truck in the window, my hand tried to tighten into a fist, forgetting that it was cupped loosely around the corpse's lower face.
>
> In that instant the truck disappeared from the window like smoke— or like the ghost I suppose it was. In the same instant I heard an awful *squirting* noise. Hot liquid filled my hand. I looked down, and saw, and that was when I began to scream. Oil was leaking from the corners of his eyes like tears. Diamond Gem Oil—the recycled stuff you can buy in a five-gallon plastic container, the stuff McCutcheon had always run in the Cresswell. (392)

The short story "Battleground" is another example of a morality tale likewise focusing on retribution for an individual's personal misconduct. The story's only human character, Renshaw, lives an affluent and complacent existence on his revenues as a professional assassin: "A Human Hawk, constructed by both genetics and environment to do two things superbly:

kill and survive" (117). Returning from his most recent assignment, Renshaw is confronted with a battalion of small toy soldiers dispatched to his luxurious suite from the mother of his latest victim. The toy invaders are ironic parallels to both the literal and philosophical view of humanity, "crawling beetle-like in the streets...the cramped and dirty tenements" (118), that Renshaw maintains from atop his penthouse terrace. The assassin operates from a fiercely independent perspective—in the literal commission of his assignments as well as in his view of how the world operates. The ensuing battle between this collection of miniature mercenaries and an adult human being has much in common with the visual effects of the film *King Kong*, as Renshaw is pursued by tiny helicopters shooting needle-like machine gun bullets. But unlike Kong, who is always more victim than victimizer, the reader feels no similar sympathetic response toward Renshaw. There remains a kind of poetic justice in his fate: destroyed at his own profession by plastic men who, like the hit-man himself, are devoid of conscience and pity.

King's version of the moral allegory owes its formulation to, and is once again reminiscent of, the romance tradition in nineteenth and twentieth-century American literature. Typically, the tales of Poe, Hawthorne, Lovecraft, Wilbur Daniel Steele, Shirley Jackson, Anne Rivers Siddons, and Flannery O'Connor, whose profound influences King acknowledges in interviews and throughout *Danse Macabre*, revolve around characters who violate standards for personal moral conduct and bring about their own self-destruction. Poe's troubled narrators, Hawthorne's egocentric scientist-intellectuals, Siddons' quasi-sophisticated suburbanites, and O'Connor's southern materialists and rationalists all share a similar disintegration of personality due in no small part to their failure to treat other human beings with sympathy and respect. In the fiction of all these authors, when a character indulges his or her basest impulses, self-annihilation is inevitable. The spirit of selfishness which is ordained in all of us from the inheritance of original sin must be kept in check or else we become monsters. Only through a conscious act of self-discipline is it possible to overcome the beast within and attain a larger spiritual capacity. The individual is presented with the choice of selfishness or selflessness. With the former comes isolation and damnation and with the latter, moral salvation.

One of the most important similarities that King's fiction shares with Shirley Jackson's *The Haunting of Hill House* is the awareness that there are always more rational and less destructive options available to the characters. A tension is often created over the issue of choice: a more rational and self-disciplined course of behavior as opposed to an acceptance of and surrender to the persuasive powers of the supernatural. Jackson's Eleanor can choose either to go away from Hill House and to try to use her new social confidence to make a life for herself, or she can give in to the house and make her home there for an eternity. Because she is so afraid of being alone again, and because Hill House has played directly to this fear, she chooses the supernatural and surrenders to the house. Similar situations are created in King's books. In *Christine*, Arnie could destroy his Plymouth and continue to live a relatively normal life with Dennis and Leigh, or he could give into Christine's demands for total devotion and complete revenge on "the shitters." He chooses, as does Eleanor, to take the easier, destructive, and anti-social course, primarily because the supernatural force that is pursuing him has played directly to his strongest weaknesses and fears: his loneliness and lack of self-esteem.

In *The Haunting of Hill House*, Dr. Montague argues that " 'no ghost in all the long histories of ghosts has ever hurt anyone physically. The only damage done is by the victim to himself.... The menace of the supernatural is that it attacks where modern minds are weakest' " (139-140). The formulation that the victim's psychological orientation is essential for the supernatural to exert any controlling effect is the single most important theme that King shares in common with Jackson. The belief that evil forces can exploit the inherent weaknesses of the human personality and probe it until the individual's identity is completely warped, dates back at least to Puritan literature. As King agrees with this essential philosophical formulation, that we inhabit a fallen world in less than perfect circumstances, his characters are always susceptible to the initial attractiveness of evil, to performing acts of personal cruelty and injustice. King's fiction likewise suggests that when human beings allow their own individual or collective impulses to proceed unchecked, a series of catastrophic events— usually completely out of human control—must necessarily ensue. These events conclude in a level of destruction and chaos commensurate with the reader's capacity for terror. Perhaps this is one possible explanation for King's dramatic talent at creating sympathetic characters.

The people in his narratives bear much in common with the rest of us: often well-intentioned, but nonetheless capable of producing catastrophic results. Dr. Louis Creed in the novel *Pet Sematary* is a case in point. Creed shares many similarities with Hawthorne's idealistic searchers: Alymer ("The Birthmark"), Rappaccini ("Rappaccini's Daughter"), Goodman Brown ("Young Goodman Brown"), Ethan Brand, and Hollingsworth (*The Blithedale Romance*). Like them, Creed fails to acknowledge (his own Unpardonable Sin) the inviolable distinction separating human idealism from the limitations of reality. The doctor refuses to heed the cryptic warning he receives in a dream from Victor Pascow, a student who has died in his arms. " 'Don't go beyond; no matter how much you feel the need to. The barrier was not meant to be broken' " (70). Instead of recognizing and accepting the dominion of death, Creed seeks to repudiate it by summoning Church, the family cat, and finally his own child and wife back from the grave. As Douglas Winter argues persuasively, "Creed, like Church, is named with intention; his creed—rationality—is the flaw that pushes him along the path to destruction. He has apparently acquired the ultimate skill of his profession as physician—the ability to return the dead to life—and he cannot help but use it" (134). Creed's quest to circumvent the design of Fate succeeds only in perverting life and his own healing skills, as he untethers the malevolent spirit-being of the ancient Indian Wendigo. His son, Gage, returns to his father, but he resembles nothing of the little boy so desperately missed: "It was not Louis's son returned from the grave but some hideous monster" (344). The resurrected Gage is a reflection of Creed's own imprudent quest and deepest human failings. The name "Gage," then, comes finally to signify the full degree of the doctor's misguided urges, which are perhaps best measured by the fact that Creed's obsession with bringing his son back to life is indulged at the expense of his other, nearly catatonic child and desolate wife: "There had been times in the dark watches of the night when she [his wife] had longed to hate Louis for the grief he had fathered inside her, and for not giving her the comfort she needed (or allowing her to give the comfort she needed to give)" (324).

Pet Sematary is a novel about secrets. King begins this haunting saga by informing us that the men who buried Hitler, popes, and kings before them, were silent about their tasks: "Death is a mystery and burial a secret." Each of the characters who appears in *Pet Sematary* serves as an illustration of this opening perspective: Louis Creed and Jud Crandall participate in and carefully maintain the dark secret of Micmac resurrections; the town of Ludlow keeps the land secret from outsiders; Victor Pascow warns against the secret powers inherent in this unholy Indian ground; Rachel Creed and her parents share the "dirty secret" of Zelda's final months of "foul, hateful, screaming...in the backroom" (180); while Ellie Creed is left to inherit the awful secrets of her father's late-night handiwork with pick and shovel. All of these death secrets are either hidden or denied, in a manner similar to the way in which the funeral director and Jud steer Creed away from the white swinging door in the mortuary basement separating a living father from his dead son (209). Only in the stony soil up in the old Micmac burial ground are any of these secrets acknowledged and indulged. As Jud Crandall observes in reflecting on the enchanted place:

"You do it because it gets hold of you. You do it because that burial place is a secret place, and you want to share the secret, and when you find a reason that seems good enough, why...then you just go ahead and do it. You make up reasons...they seem like good reasons...but mostly you do it because you want to. Or because you have to." (146)

The novel abounds in spiral and circular shapes and patterns: the concentric circle of graves in the Pet Sematary itself; the stone stairs that wind ever deeper into the woods leading to the rocky plateau of the Micmac burial site, and there revealing yet another circle of crypts; Victor Pascow's recurring image in the foreboding dreamscapes of Louis and Ellie Creed; and ultimately the revolving identities subsumed by the liberated Wendigo, covering a nightmarish review of the novel's cast of characters, in its transmogrification of Gage Creed. Doctor Creed's evolving awareness of these symbolic shapes begins as early as his introduction to the Pet Sematary, when he notices that "the circular pattern, perceived as an almost haphazard coincidence in the outer rows, was very evident" (30-1). As his involvement with the forces in the Micmac burial ground deepens, his sense of the circle's significance likewise enlarges to cosmic proportions. Standing aside his son's fresh grave, contemplating whether to risk disinterment for reburial in the Micmac ground, Louis apprehends the full meaning of the spiral's relationship to the Pet Sematary: "The graves in the Pet Sematary mimed

the most ancient religious symbol of all: diminishing circles
indicating a spiral down, not to a point, but to infinity....The
spiral was the oldest sign of power in the world, man's oldest
symbol of that twisty bridge which may exist between the world
and the Gulf" (256-7). The image of the spiral has many mystical
significances in Indian lore, especially; it often suggests the
twisted, the devious, and the tortuous. Dante was also quite
consciously aware of the symbolic properties of geometric forms
as he employs spiral and circular imagery throughout *The Divine
Comedy*, particularly in describing his descent into the inferno.
The spiral is therefore symbolic of a continuous fact of life: that
the wrong-doings of one man can, and soon enough, will be
the evil of the next man. Jud introduces Louis to the Micmac
graveyard and the secret of the Wendigo. By the end of the novel
Louis in turn has introduced Steve Masterton to the magnetic
powers of the site.

Once he makes his decision to move Gage, Creed is no longer
merely a detached observer of geometric symmetries, but a willing
participant in, and a connecting point for, the spiral's mystical
properties: "Louis glanced down at the raked dirt of Gage's grave
and felt a wave of awe and horror course through him.
Unknowing, moving by themselves, his fingers had drawn a
pattern in the dirt—he had drawn a spiral" (260).

In probing the secrets of death, Doctor Creed attempts to
overcome the same mortal limitations that frustrate Ellie early
in the book when she contemplates the inevitable demise of her
cat:

"Honey," he said, "if it was up to me, I'd let Church live to be a
hundred. But I don't make the rules."
"Who does?" she asked, and then, with infinite scorn: "God, I suppose."
Louis stifled the urge to laugh. It was too serious.
"God or Somebody," he said. "Clocks run down—that's all I know.
There are no guarantees, babe."
"I don't want Church to be like all those dead pets!" she burst out,
suddenly tearful and furious. "I don't want Church to ever be dead! He's
my cat! He's not God's cat! Let God have His own cat! Let God have
all the damn old cats He wants, and kill them all! Church is *mine!*" (36-
7)

The selfish rebellion that characterizes Ellie's first encounter with
the reality of death is the same response Louise Creed exhibits
when he loses his son to this force that "makes the rules," or,
in Zelda's words, "Oz the Gweat and Tewwible." After Gage

is killed, Creed's "urge to laugh" at death's seriousness is quickly abandoned, and with it disappears his rational argument that the end of life is "perfectly natural" (41). At various points throughout the book Creed appears to be keeping an unconscious personal record against death. Each time his medical skills aid in saving a human life, Creed whispers to himself "won one today, Louis" (161). However, when death deals him the decisive "defeat" of his life by literally snatching Gage from beneath his very fingertips, Creed decides to cheat the reaper, hoping to get ahead in the score again by employing the supernatural energies of the Micmac soil to reclaim his son. After the burial of Church, Jud tells Creed that "bring[ing] the dead back to life...that's about as close to playing God as you can get, ain't it?" (146). Creed's choice to play God is a violation of the natural order thesis he had earlier tried to instill within Ellie and Rachel. The doctor's refusal to accept the workings of Fate estranges him from family, friends, and community, disrupts his rational hold on existence, and transforms him into an extension of the amoral powers residing within the Wendigo.

Like some Old Testament seer extending his prophetic warning, Victor Pascow's cryptic message reverberates beyond the woods surrounding the Pet Sematary until it becomes the single most important voice in King's fictional landscape: there are certain mysteries man must simply learn to accept, certain secrets he has no business attempting to discover, and certain moral barriers that he only transcends at the expense of his soul. This is among the most recurrent of King's themes: one's humanity—or one's soul—is dreadfully easy to lose, and what we abandon ourselves to possess, we necessarily become. William Blake, two centuries earlier, may have felt perfect harmony residing in "the lineaments of gratified desire," but for King the inevitable end of such self-absorption is the madness of Louis Creed circling back for another trip to the Pet Sematary, carrying his wife's corpse wrapped in a sheet, his own howls of torment indistinguishable from the Wendigo's laugh of triumph.

3

In spite of the mechanistic world-view maintained in most gothic fiction, King's characters still possess a persuasive element of free will. The majority of his protagonists are like Louis Creed: they choose their own course of action. As Bernadette Bosky argues in "The Mind's a Monkey," "great emphasis is placed on humanity's ability to choose.... No matter what choice an individual in the story may make—even that of Harold Lauder or Jack Torrance—a world of meaningful choice is affirmed" (211). The manipulatory skills of the Wendigo notwithstanding, Doctor Creed willfully elects to spurn the repeated warnings of Jud Crandall and Victor Pascow. Creed essentially acknowledges his terrible freedom moments before he sets "Oz the Gweat and Tewwible" in motion by disinterring his son: "his heart told him quietly and absolutely that he couldn't come back tomorrow. If he didn't do it tonight, he could never do it.... This was the moment, the only time for it he was ever going to have" (297).

Similarly, those individuals who *choose* to reject social and interpersonal relationships (distinguished from characters like Carrie White, who are *forced* into isolated states) are more apt to succumb to the corrosive influence of evil, and to unleash the demons in King's netherworld. Harold Lauder in *The Stand*, Todd Bowden in *Apt Pupil*, Arnie Cunningham in *Christine*, Frank Dodd and Greg Stillson in *The Dead Zone*, Morgan Sloat in *The Talisman*, and Rainbird in *Firestarter* are divorced from any kind of genuine personal, familial, or communal affiliations. Despite their differing circumstances, all of these men have forfeited their bonds with Hawthorne's "magnetic chain of humanity," and their subsequent isolation makes them vulnerable to iniquitous behavior.

In *The Stand*, as Harold Lauder moves ever more gradually away from the community of the Boulder Free Zone (even his house is located on the outskirts of town), whatever weak commitment he once shared with the civilized values of a humanitarian existence is severed accordingly. Harold's decision to give up his chance to be "someone" in Boulder is influenced by his unrequited love for Franny, but this is not the only factor that is responsible for his behavior. The greater part of Lauder's existence reveals a boy-man partially inept, partially unwilling, to establish meaningful contact with other people. His diary entries are a nihilistic venting of antisocial frustrations. Moreover, his chronic urge to masturbate is further evidence of both his immaturity and alienation. Like the denizens of Las Vegas, who live in a perpetual state of fear and mistrust, Harold maintains a barely repressed sense of social estrangement that can be traced throughout the novel, and Franny is constantly afraid of disturbing his unstable ego.

Harold's only serious moment of self-conflict and doubt occurs when he must align himself with either those members of the Free Zone, who have come to respect his intelligence and contributions to the community (the Burial Committee nicknames him "Hawk" because of his leadership skills), or Flagg's vague pledge of great authority over the eventual destruction of the Free Zone. Lauder's decision to become Flagg's pliant agent underscores his deliberate rejection of a social identity. It is thus appropriate that Harold's death, which is the result of the Black Man's betrayal of his promise, occurs in isolation on the side of a deserted mountain. Bereft of all human companionship and solace, surrounded by desert wasteland and his life's only real sources of release, his motorcycle and writing journal, Lauder's suicide is a final reflection of his self-absorption and increasing distance from others. Like the shattered bones in his leg which leave him incapacitated on the mountain, Harold remains a splintered character, doomed because of his choice to break away from the community of men.

Larry Underwood emerges as the novel's dramatic foil to Lauder. Like Harold, Underwood's pre-plague history unfolds in a series of selfish and antisocial gestures. He barely tolerates his mother, his affection for other women extends only so far as the bedroom, and his instantaneous success as a rock star enlarges his own self-esteem to the point where it alienates his few remaining friends. Haunted by his guilt over Rita's death and the echo of an abandoned lover's final salutation, " 'you ain't no nice guy' " (75), Larry stumbles through the post-plague world resolute in his desire to transform his personality. The fact that he is repulsed whenever his hit song "Baby Can You Dig Your Man?" is mentioned or played is subtle evidence indicating the difference between the two versions of his character represented in the course of the novel. The new world refines Underwood's capacity for performing good to the same degree as it allows Harold to indulge in evil. By sinking deeper into himself, Lauder rejects the opportunity to escape the isolation that characterized his past. Underwood, on the other hand, learns the importance of self-discipline and love. In spurning Nadine's sexual seduction (Chapter 43), Larry demonstrates a newly found capacity for self-control, a willingness to avoid causing Lucy pain, and both of these qualities stand in marked contrast to Harold's physical and mental vulnerability. Finally, where Lauder remains obsessed with the urge to annihilate whatever he cannot dominate, Underwood never allows the various leadership roles he assumes (and always at the urging of others) to defile his evolving personality; indeed, at the end of the novel his self-sacrifice becomes the means by which others are able to survive.

4

Evil exhibits itself everywhere in King's cosmos as something negative, barren, weakening, a principle of death. It isolates, disunites, and tends to annihilate not only its opposite but itself. When a King character is mastered by evil, it destroys other people through him, but it also destroys him. At the close of the struggle the character, like Randall Flagg in *The Stand*, vanishes, leaving behind him nothing that endures.

King tells us that evil can be resisted—indeed, many of his characters do so successfully—but those who are attracted to, and ultimately subsumed within, impenetrable malevolent forces are doomed precisely because of their own failure to recognize and regulate corresponding urges within themselves. As powerful a principle as evil is in King's universe, it can establish dominion only at the expense of the individual's moral conscience, and King further postulates that this cannot occur unless the individual allows it.

In one of the most compelling and horrifying novels King has written to date, *The Shining*, the Overlook Hotel seems to have had an evil attraction from its onset, as though a malevolent *genius loci* were present. From its iniquitous origins, the hotel has apparently been accumulating and concentrating instances of human evil. It thus owes at least part of its perverse psychic energies to a long and unsavory history of human sin: "Men reputed to be involved with drugs, vice, robbery, murder.... Every hotel has its ghost? The Overlook had a whole coven of them. First suicide, then the Mafia, what next?" (163). One of the subtle, and certainly most important, facets of the book is that the Overlook is only capable of exerting influence over its caretakers—first Delbert Grady, then Jack Torrance—by exploiting their personal weaknesses which were manifest long before either man accepted the job as caretaker. As King observes in *Danse Macabre*, "I began to wonder if the haunted house could not be turned into a kind of symbol of unexpiated sin...an idea which turned out to be pivotal in the novel *The Shining*" (253). In Jack's case, which is, of course, the central focus of the book, the hotel methodically assaults his very identity, stimulating a myriad of self-doubts and anxieties: a strained relationship with his wife and child, tendencies toward violence and self-pity, vivid memories of an abusive father, a struggle against alcoholism, and the quest to become a successful writer. Danny perceives Jack's conflicts intuitively from the beginning of the novel:

His daddy hurt almost all the time, mostly about the Bad Thing. Danny could almost always pick that up too: Daddy's craving to go into a dark place and watch a color TV and eat peanuts out of a bowl and do the Bad Thing until his brain would be quiet and leave him alone.... The wanting, the *needing* to get drunk had never been so bad. His hands shook. He knocked things over. And he kept wanting to take it out on Wendy and Danny. His temper was like a vicious animal on a frayed leash. (28, 37)

In "The Life and Death of Richard Bachman," Stephen Brown cites King's evaluation of the novel *Thinner*: "[It] is a story about responsibilities. It's about coming to grips with your responsibilities and what happens when you don't. If you avoid your obligations, then you always end up hurting your loved ones" (125). The theme of human accountability for personal actions is not exclusive to the novel *Thinner*; in fact, King's comment is even more applicable to *The Shining*. Although Jack often appears to be helplessly trapped in the mechanistic design of the Overlook and by the soft determinism of his own warped past, his decision to render the snowmobile—their only avenue of escape—unworkable (Chapter 33) is a choice he makes in complete awareness of the hotel's evil purpose and with the full understanding that he is endangering his family. Jack's selfish motivations—" 'I wouldn't allow my son to make decisions concerning my career' " (351)—always keep him from acting in a responsible manner. In this pivotal scene, Jack willfully decides to abandon his personal struggles and obligations to indulge his self-destructive tendencies. From this point on, his destiny becomes one with the hotel's: "he looked like an absurd twentieth-century Hamlet, an indecisive figure so mesmerized by the onrushing tragedy that he was helpless to divert its course or alter it in any way" (297). The glass-domed, wind-up clock Danny discovers in the ballroom (Chapter 37) is a metaphor for the Torrances' situation at the Overlook: Jack's moral deficiencies are the keys which wind the gothic machinery of the hotel into motion, leaving the Torrance family susceptible to its sinister machinations. "Supernatural intervention," argues Bosky, "particularly malefic forces[,] can only occur because the character possesses those tendencies and yields to the corresponding influences" (225).

The Overlook is a parasitic organism, growing more powerful as it ingests human malfeasance. It seems to comprehend immediately that Jack is the most assailable member of the Torrance family: "It wasn't Danny who was the weak link, it was him. He was the vulnerable one, the one who could be bent and twisted until something snapped" (278-9). With the exception of the ballroom party revellers, who appear late in the novel and are designed to intimidate more than to captivate, the Overlook's menacing energies virtually ignore Wendy. Jack's infatuation with the beautiful woman in the ballroom (Chapter 44), "tall and auburn-haired, dressed in clinging white satin, dancing close to him, her breasts pressed softly and sweetly against his chest," is an appropriate symbol for the hotel's relationship to its current caretaker. Under the seductive cloak of loveliness and the promise of decadent pleasures, lurks the reality of manipulation and decay. As Jack is aroused by the "smooth-and-powdered nakedness under her dress," he is also simultaneously cognizant that the ghost-woman's breath is fouled by the scent of the grave's corruption: "like lilies, secret and hidden in cracks furred with green moss—places where sunshine is short and shadows long" (346).

When the original manuscript of *The Shining* was first submitted for publication, King had included about a hundred more pages elaborating upon the sordid history of the Overlook and its principal owners, all of whom were enslaved and eventually doomed by the hotel's perverse charms. This material, cut by King's editor at Doubleday to reduce the overall length of the book, has only recently surfaced under the published title "Before the Play." Aside from detailing many of the violent acts committed at the Overlook since its opening, King's expunged prologue is unified by the similar experiences shared by these three early owners. Each man's commitment to the Overlook was monolithic, even in the face of bankruptcies, divorce, and death. For all of them—Bob T. Watson, James Parris, and Horace Derwent—the Overlook radiated the same feminine allure that mesmerizes Jack Torrance. This deadly attraction gradually merged into obsession; and as each man's rapture intensified, the owners' wives and lovers, paralleling Wendy Torrance's relationship with Jack, lost the affection of their men and became subject to abuse and neglect:

Bob T. had fallen in love with the hotel as an idea, and his love had deepened as the hotel took shape, no longer a mental thing but an actual edifice with strong, clean lines and infinite possibility. His wife had grown to hate it—at one point in 1908 she told him that she would have preferred competing with another woman, that at least she would have known how to cope with—but he had dismissed her hate as a hysterical female reaction to Boyd's [their son] death on the grounds. (20-1)

Just as the Overlook's owners in turn became owned by the Overlook, the hotel eventually becomes Jack Torrance's spiritual caretaker, representing a composite of his darkest motivations, and further subverting his tenuous familial bonds. Already self-absorbed before he even sets foot in the hotel, by the end of the novel Jack has descended completely into himself. His morbid self-awareness corresponds to and is encouraged by his progressively deeper involvement with the hotel. This is a novel of contraction: as the snow flies, the environment becomes ever more circumscribed, narrowing into specific moments of the hotel's historical decadence and viciousness (e.g. the masquerade party) which are accompanied by the ghosts of its most odious human personalities. This sense of the hotel's narrowing restrictiveness finds a parallel in Jack's behavior, as he moves further away from his commitment to writing, his dedication to Danny, and whatever affection he shared with Wendy, and toward refining the meanness that has always been a part of the darker side of his personality. As he becomes more obsessed with the Overlook's corrupt history, his attitude toward Wendy and Danny deteriorates proportionately. The most unnerving aspects of this genuinely frightening book are less associated with the phantoms that haunt the Overlook than with the erosion of Jack's relationship to his family. His verbal harangues against Wendy escalate into violent physical confrontations. In place of the reciprocal love which once informed their marriage, Jack reduces their union to a mirror of his own mental anguish.

King reserves, however, his greatest assault upon the reader's sensibilities for the demise of Jack's relationship with Danny. Early in the book we learn of Danny's unqualified love for his father: "She had stuck with Jack more for Danny's sake than she would admit in her waking hours, but now, sleeping lightly, she could admit it: Danny had been Jack's for the asking, almost from the first" (53). Jack's association with Danny is a perverse parallel to the biblical story of Abraham and Isaac. Instead of sacrificing his son to prove his loyalty to the Will of God, Jack stalks Danny to ingratiate himself with the ruling hierarchy of the hotel. The Overlook's monomania with Danny becomes Jack's, trapping him into an ever more circumscribed and narrowing arena of his own mind, finally unable to separate himself from the hotel's labyrinthine hallways and dark recesses: "Nothing in the Overlook frightened him. He felt that he and it were *simpatico*" (251).

Although King has voiced his own dissatisfaction with its cinematic adaptation, the portrayal of Torrance's mental confinement and anguish is the most effective visual statement developed in Stanley Kubrick's version of *The Shining*. As I understand them, King's major points of contention are with Kubrick's failure to represent adequately the novel's layers of complexity and, most important, to uphold its overall dramatic structure. Essentially, King feels as though Kubrick has rewritten his book for him, which is not altogether untrue. But on the issue of representing Jack Torrance's breakdown in a systematic and thoroughly convincing manner, Kubrick cannot be faulted.

Thomas Allen Nelson has written an interesting film study, *Kubrick: Inside An Artist's Maze*, that traces maze imagery throughout Kubrick's work. In his chapter on *The Shining*, Nelson argues that the movie's maze concept suggests the psychological doublings of character and meaning that are at the heart of the film. Through several close mis-en-scene analyses, Nelson demonstrates that Kubrick's reliance on color blends, character juxtapositions, mirror effects, and fragmented time sequences produces a "process of reduction and intensification which moves toward a single moment in time when insanity breaks loose from the bonds of rational order" (211). Kubrick's reliance on a series of restated labyrinthine images is used to underscore Jack's deterioration throughout the film. Like the image of the spiral that appears as a metaphor for Louis Creed's de-evolution into the evil of the Micmac burial ground, the abundant maze imagery in Kubrick's *The Shining* reflects Jack Torrance's entrapment in a malevolent universe. The Indian rug patterns on the Overlook's floors and walls, the hotel's excruciatingly long corridors exaggerated by the use of a wide-angle lens camera, the maze of words that Jack types into various convoluted forms on sheets of paper, and even Danny's line of snow-prints that eventually lead his father deep within the hedge maze outside the hotel—all of these images of enclosure are metaphors for the encroaching perimeters of Jack's mind. Moreover, they all coalesce into the film's concluding scene: a final maze pattern, consisting of wall photographs representing the Overlook's history. Jack Torrance's smiling face is, of course, appropriately centered in the middle of the collection. Significantly, Jack elects to remain inside the hotel's corridors and rooms (especially within the Colorado Lounge, which appears to be the center of the Overlook's "brain") while Wendy and Danny are free to explore its outdoor surroundings. Until the final chase through the snow-encrusted hedge maze, Jack is never seen outside of the hotel's interiors; in maintaining this limited perspective, Kubrick suggests that Torrance is physically and mentally locked within the hotel.

If Kubrick is to be remonstrated for his rendition of *The Shining*, it must be for his unwillingness to recreate any texture of the historical evil that informs King's novel, and to which the latter devotes enough attention so that the individual pasts of his protagonists merge into the collective past of the Overlook. While the film remains devoted to Jack's *present* (as Nelson has already reminded us, "that moment in time when insanity breaks loose"), King's novel enriches the meaning of this breakdown through frequent references to Jack's *past*. The novel connects Jack's tendencies toward violence and extending punishment for his own mistakes to others with his father's alcoholism and history of corporeal abuse. Moreover, Wendy's failure to assert her independence from Jack until it is almost too late is explained in her relationship to her mother. The latter established and encouraged Wendy's feelings of insecurity and self-depreciating pattern of dependency. Thus, while Kubrick's film lacks the contextual explanations for events which transpire at the Overlook, King's novel, by contrast, is all the more terrifying because of their inclusion. The writer's careful attention to tracing three generations of father-son doublings in *The Shining* effectively locates the genesis of Jack Torrance's corruption within patterns of learned human behavior, and in so doing forces a level of reader comprehension and identification that is unavailable in Kubrick's ahistorical adaptation.

5

In the destruction of the Torrance father-son bond, King exploits one of humankind's deepest primal fears: that we are unwanted by our parents, repulsive to our children. If a father can turn against his innocent son so totally, then there is nothing inviolable in the universe; nothing is secure; and there is no basis for faith. *The Shining* reveals a vision of worldly darkness that rivals Shakespeare's *King Lear* in its intensity and in its breakup of the social foundations which codify Western civilization. King has noted in an essay written after the novel's publication entitled "On *The Shining* and Other Perpetrations," that his book was originally conceived and structured "in the form of a five-act Shakespearean tragedy" (14). Indeed, Jack Torrance shares much in common with the Shakespearean tragic hero. Like Torrance, Shakespeare's kings and warriors fall from grace in large part as a result of their own choice of behavior. The Shakespearean hero is endowed with a certain degree of free will and his actions are, to some extent, responsible for the catastrophe that eventually befalls him. On the other hand, as A.C. Bradley points out in his book *Shakespearean Tragedy*, while the tragic hero acts freely, we sense that, at certain crucial points, he is helpless to alter the course of his destruction (19). There is, in other words, always a certain degree of powerlessness in the hands of a larger Fate which works against the tragic hero's welfare (e.g. Desdemona loses her handkerchief at just the wrong time in *Othello*; the delay that costs Cordelia her life in *Lear*). Jack Torrance's tragic fall in *The Shining* shows both of these tendencies at work: his character flaws are exploited by a greater design (the forces at the Overlook) actively engaged in bringing about his destruction.

When Jack is abandoned by his wife and child, he closely resembles one of Shakespeare's self-destructing tragic heroes— Macbeth or Tidus Andronicus—insofar as his madness makes him no longer recognizable as a human being. His face "lathered in blood, the single eye tiny and piggish and glittering," his once articulate language reduced to incoherent howls and mindless repetition of the phrase "come out and take your medicine," Jack is transformed into "a strange, shifting composite" of the abominable creatures who populate the Overlook (429). And as a final point of comparison, after the Shakespearean tragic hero falls, the whole universe is shaken. What usually remains is an exhausted city or family that re-establishes life's order in a manner similar to the last pages of *The Shining*.

Like the demonic metamorphosis which takes place in Louis Creed at the conclusion of *Pet Sematary*, Jack Torrance has relinquished his body, as well as his mind, to powers that ultimately betray him. Both men become appendicular versions of the Wendigo. Having failed in his responsibilities to himself— to his teaching, to his writing, and to the welfare of his family— Torrance accepts the only duty for which he is now truly qualified:

caretaker of the heinous specters. In his terrible isolation, uncontrolled fury, and impending doom, he becomes an appropriate extension of the hotel itself, "a flaming pyre in the roaring throat of the night" (438). The most loathsome monsters in King's canon, as is the case as well in Dante's *Inferno*, are always partially human; they represent the twisting of human tendencies and desires until these desires become bestial, connected by only a remote resemblance to the rest of humanity.

Throughout the greater part of Stephen King's fiction, once again reminiscent of Shakespeare, is a tremendous sense of violation and upheaval. King appears to imply that the Faustian quest to be greater than what is mortally possible paves the way for corruption of the individual. In King, individuals betray one another's trust, oppressive societal structures and organizations seek to impose their will over others, personal pasts and family histories pervert and eventually dominate the present, and innocent lives are irrevocably changed by supernatural intrusions. For each of these representative categories there are a myriad of specific examples from King's work. It is likewise possible to affiliate the names of several adolescent characters with each of the above fictional contexts. In fact, it is most often King's children who must accept the consequences of adult moral lapses. For example, we can only speculate about the dark futures awaiting Danny Torrance and Ellie Creed, their young lives deeply scarred by their fathers' transgressions. The next three chapters consider the importance of children in King's moral scheme. His young people, like the majority of his adults, are often cast in the role of victim—violated by corrupt social institutions, inherited sins, and adult codes of immoral behavior. Other adolescents in his work, however, somehow manage to endure. Those who do, seem aided by their commitment to traditional virtues that affirm the sanctity of human life even in the face of its violation.

Chapter 5
Inherited Haunts:
Stephen King's Terrible Children

At the closing address of the 1984 International Conference on the Fantastic in Arts, someone in the audience asked Stephen King the question, "What terrifies you the most?" King's reply was emphatic and immediate: "Opening the door of my children's bedroom and finding one of them dead."

King's dread that his own offspring can be harmed has not inhibited his use of infantile and adolescent characters who more often than not find themselves in precarious situations. His youthful protagonists are besieged by a variety of demons and ghosts, religious extremists and officials representing an assortment of institutions and bureaucracies. Against these oppressive legions, King's children are often endowed with uncommon powers and traits, and these special attributes, combined with a native shrewdness and acute perceptivity, help distinguish them from the adult world while aiding in their survival.

King's most memorable and important characters, and the ones to whom we, as readers, grow increasingly attached, are his children. Most of his fictional adolescents find themselves enmeshed in the dark complexities of an adult world; they are not responsible for either their parents' divorces or governmental errors in judgment, but they are nonetheless forced into coping with the consequences of such events. The writer chooses to place them at the locus of so many of his books because their physical size and worldly unsophistication make them exceptionally vulnerable. King's children, like the female protagonist in one of Mrs. Ann Radcliff's eighteenth-century gothic novels, are perfect victims—their confrontations with evil initially appear overwhelming—and their plights elicit intensely sympathetic responses from the reader. Moreover, the child's heightened sensitivities and imagination put him in a position where fear consists of definite textures and smells untempered by the mechanisms of denial and rationality.

The long-term influence of childhood guilt and anxiety is a fundamental component of the psychological horror story. But this emphasis is not restricted to the horror genre. One thinks immediately of Pip in Dickens' *Great Expectations*, whose adult life is irrevocably shaped by the terrifying events of his childhood. Many of King's tales probe the relationship between childhood fears and adult neuroses. In the short story "The Monkey," a wind-up toy monkey is associated with the violent events and subsequent guilt of Hal Shelburn's adolescence. Nearly half the story is narrated in flashback sequences to various moments of Hal's childhood, and these scenes are unified by the monkey's clanging cymbals as a prologue to someone's death. Since the toy is discovered by Hal and his brother "all the way down at the far end of the back closet" in his parents' bedroom (151), the monkey becomes a metaphor for Hal's most vivid childhood recollections; it represents that part of his subconscious mind which is unable to overcome the events of his tragic youth: a father who abandons him at an early age, his mother's sudden brain embolism, and pets and childhood friends who abruptly die. As Hal, now an adult with sons of his own, discovers one morning in his hotel room when he awakens to find the monkey mysteriously nestling against his face, the creature is an undeniable aspect of Hal himself, symbolizing the dark window of anxiousness that looks back on his past: "There was the guilt; the certain, deadly knowledge that he had killed his mother by winding the monkey up on that sunny after-school afternoon" (158-9).

It is significant that the toy's re-emergence from the deep well in which Hal entombed it twenty years earlier coincides with another series of personal traumas: the death of Hal's Aunt Ida, the loss of a prestigious job, his wife's serious addiction to valium, and his son's growing disaffection. The tragic events occurring to Hal as an adult cannot be separated from his adolescent memories. As a child Hal sought to bury his guilt and neuroses by twice returning the monkey to its box back in the closet and eventually by dropping it to the bottom of an abandoned well. Each time he rids himself of the monkey, his dark recollections are correspondingly silenced. But in order to accomplish this, on each separate occasion he must bury the monkey in a deeper place, an indication of the increasing psychological assault taking place against his consciousness. In finally sinking the monkey in "the deepest part of Crystal Lake" (167), Hal reasserts control over his anxieties by symbolically resubmerging them into the unfathomable recesses of his psyche. Surmounting the life-threatening storm that almost kills him on the lake, his triumphant reunion with his son on the placid shore is an indication that Hal has broken from the childhood pattern of guilt and anxiety now threatening his adulthood.

1

In King's fiction, children embody the full spectrum of human experience; they are identified with the extremes of good and evil. Many of his youthful protagonists come to represent the moral centers of his books and from them all other actions seem to radiate. Some represent the nucleus for familial love. They are often healing forces, as in the first halves of *The Shining*, *Pet Sematary*, and *Cujo*, enabling parents in unstable marriages to forgive one another's human failings. Moreover, King is inordinately fond of testing the moral capacities of his adolescent protagonists. Mark Petrie (*'Salem's Lot*) and Jack Sawyer (*The Talisman*) encounter tremendous adversities and defeats, yet each boy refuses to capitulate to powers vastly superior to his own. As a result of their endurance they not only manage to survive, but also to prevail. Many of King's children represent the principle of good in a corrupt world; they seem both divinely inspired and painfully cursed with prophetic knowledge. Danny Torrance, Carrie White, and Charlie McGee possess superhuman abilities that trigger death and destruction, and yet these children elicit a positive response from us because they are so thoroughly manipulated and abused. It is not really the children who are responsible for their various acts of destruction, but the adults who mislead and torment them.

At the other moral pole are the adolescent hunters—the denim fascists in "Sometimes They Come Back," *Christine*, and *Carrie*—who portray ambassadors from an immoral world, their sole purpose being to wreak destruction on anyone or anything weaker than or different from themselves. One of King's greatest fortes remains his ability to render the most perverse and grotesque aspects of the American high school experience with unflinching accuracy. King's descriptions of the public school system are so concrete and identifiable that they must have been shaped by his own brief exposure to the teaching profession as a high school English instructor. The majority of students and teachers who appear in his books care little about education or the transference of knowledge; his teachers are shell-shocked veterans on the verge of surrendering to a student body that lacks both personal and academic discipline. His modern public schools are sterile environments, without spirit or mystery, devoid of transcendence. As King points out in *Danse Macabre* in the context of a discussion about *Carrie*:

> ...the book tries to deal with the loneliness of one girl, her desperate effort to become a part of the peer society in which she must exist, and how her effort fails. If it had any thesis to offer, this deliberate updating of *High School Confidential*, it was that high school is a place of almost bottomless conservatism and bigotry, a place where the adolescents who attend are no more allowed to rise "above their station" than a Hindu would be allowed to rise above his or her caste. (169)

In *Carrie*, King works from a bifurcated perspective in analyzing this setting for adolescent violence. On one hand, he understands that Carrie White's night of revenge is motivated by the brutality of her classmates. On the other hand, his exoneration of Carrie is equalled in his contempt for the boy-men, girl-women who torment her. King's truest sympathies are always with the high school rejects; they are not only victimized by the cruelty of the majority, but because of their status as pariahs they often possess a level of intelligence and sensitivity sadly missing in their more popular peers. As King continues in *Danse Macabre*, "Against such a backdrop, Carrie becomes doubly pitiful, because...she can only wait to be saved or damned by the actions of others. Her only power is her telekinetic ability, and both book and movie eventually arrive at the same point: Carrie uses her 'wild talent' to pull down the whole rotten society" (172).

King seems most unfavorably inclined toward the superficially well-adjusted, popular student with an overly active libido and a underdeveloped value system. His class presidents, football quarterbacks, and prom queens bear an unmistakable resemblance to the street punks who attend the same school system as a stopover on their way to jail: both groups of adolescents have completely severed their bonds with childhood innocence. In their vicious lust to exploit sex, alcohol, and violence (for they inhabit an exclusively physical plane of existence), their behavior is modeled on an extreme conception of adulthood. They want all the pleasure of worldly experience, with none of the responsibilities. Thus, they are simply young versions of the corruption which animates King's adult society. If they manage to live long enough, they will become the Jack Torrances, Morgan Sloats, John Rainbirds, and Greg Stillsons of the next generation.

2

The adults in King's fiction act frequently like the worst of his children; they explore places where they have no business going, their behavior is often immature and without conscience, and, as we have seen elsewhere in this book, their institutions— the church, the state's massive bureaucratic system of control, the nuclear family itself—barely mask an undercurrent of violence that is capable of manifesting itself at any given moment. The daily interactions in their marriages and neighborhoods bring out the evil in King's adult characters; they revert to the meanness of adolescence, acknowledging their selfish urges only after they have set in motion a series of events which lead to catastrophe. In order to circumvent such disasters, King's children must cling to their youthful idealism and romantic innocence, both of which come under fierce attack in his fiction from the oppressive forces of societal institutions and/or the supernatural monsters who emerge as a consequence of adult moral lapses. In *Danse Macabre*, King maintains a sharp distinction, as he does throughout his fictional canon, between the worlds of the child and the adult:

The drinking age in Maine was then eighteen (booze-related accidents on the highways have since caused the lawmakers to move the age up to twenty), and all of those people [in a bar] had looked about eighteen to me. So I got up and asked the bouncer how he knew that last guy was underage. He shrugged. "You just know," he said. "It's mostly in their eyes."

For weeks after, my hobby was looking at the faces of adults and trying to decide exactly what it was that made them "adult faces." The face of a thirty-year-old is healthy, unwrinkled, and no bigger than the face of a seventeen-year-old. Yet you know that's no kid; you *know*. There seems to be some hidden yet overriding characteristic that makes what we all agree is the Adult Face. It isn't just the clothes or the stance, it isn't the fact that the thirty-year-old is toting a briefcase and the seventeen-year-old is toting a knapsack; if you put the head of each in one of those carnival cut-outs which show the body of a capering sailor or a prize-fighter, you could still pick out the adult ten tries out of ten.

I came to believe that the bouncer was right. It's in the eyes.

Not something that's there; something, rather, that has left.... The imagination is an eye, a marvelous eye that floats free. As children, that eye sees with 20/20 clarity. As we grow older, its vision begins to dim....
(378)

While it may be difficult to explain the exact "something that has left" in the adult consciousness, King seems to share a strong sympathy with William Wordsworth's emphasis on the differences separating child from adult. In *The Prelude* and throughout most of his major poems, Wordsworth argues that the secrets of existence are hidden from the adult, but the child, because she has lived for so short a time, is still close to the state of pre-existence. As the child grows into the adult, innocence and purity are tempered by a sense of loss, and her perception is no longer unified, but dualized. The child responds to the world with an instinctive joy and with the innocence of a pure soul. Wordsworth further believed that the child could serve as a guide for the adult, teaching the mature man or woman to use his or her own memory of youth to uncover the continuity of existence. As he remarked in "My Heart Leaps Up,"

The Child is the father of the Man;
And I could wish my days to be
Bound each to each by natural piety.

While King adheres closely to Wordsworth's conception of the differences between child and adult, he seldom shares the romantic poet's confidence in the ability of the adult to recapture the "natural piety" of the child. In fact, in spite of their good will and special gifts, King's children are shaped and motivated by the adults who are deeply absorbed in a personal struggle with evil. There are notable exceptions, of course, and we will consider them in the next chapter, but most often King's young people—Gage Creed, Danny Torrance, Carrie White, and Charlie McGee—exercise very little influence over the adults who continue on a self-directed course of destruction. These children are instead forced to pay for their parents' sins of curiosity and selfishness; their innocence becomes the price for an intimate examination of evil.

The short story "Children of the Corn" is a case in point. A young couple, their marriage in disarray, stumble upon Gatlin, Nebraska, a town where time has apparently stopped. Instead of August 1976, Burt and Vicky discover calendars and municipal records that go no further than 1964: "Something had happened in 1964. Something to do with religion, and corn...and children" (268). Moreover, there are no adults in this town, only children under the age of nineteen.

The time period is certainly of crucial significance to the story's meaning. But King never completely explains its mystery. Nor is it clear immediately why all the adults have been killed and why no child is permitted to survive past the age of nineteen. Like Vicky and Burt, the reader is supplied only with information about an Old Testament Jehovah whom the children worship in the corn fields. In return for their human sacrifices, he invests the crop with a special purity: "In the last of the daylight [Burt] swept his eyes closely over the row of corn to his left. And he saw that every leaf and stalk was perfect, which was just not possible. No yellow blight. No tattered leaves, no caterpillar eggs, no burrows" (275).

Reading King's best fiction is often like visiting a unfamiliar city with innumerable corners of intriguing complexity and atmospheres that reward prolonged observation. "Children of the Corn" encourages the reader to linger over multiple interpretations. On the most obvious level, it is a story of religious fanaticism dedicated to a malevolent deity. But such a reading does not account for the importance of the 1964 time setting— the initial period of active involvement by American forces in Vietnam—and its relationship to the fertility of the Nebraska corn. They appear irrevocably linked. Listening to the radio outside of town, Vicky and Burt hear a child's voice: " 'There's some that think it's okay to get out in the world, as if you could work and walk in the world without being smirched by the world' " (256). And later in the story, after he has learned the awful secret of the town, Burt wonders if human sacrifices were ordained because the corn was dying as a result of too much sinning (268).

Although King is cautious to avoid so overt a nexus, the reader with any sense of history will recall the violation of the land in Vietnam by such toxic chemicals as Agent Orange. Man's technology carried the poisoning of the soil, not to mention the levels of death and carnage, to the point at which the land itself (symbolized in the presence of the corn god) demanded repentance. If we place the events of this story in such a context, it becomes possible to understand why all the adults past the (draft) age of nineteen are sacrificed. These are the individuals who were most responsible for the war, for the "adult sins" that defiled and destroyed acres of Vietnamese landscape, thousands of American and Vietnamese lives, and, finally, what was left of America's innocence. For Vietnam was, among other things, America's collective cultural emergence into the "adult world" of sin and error. Our loss of innocence and our recognition of self-corruption is what gave impetus to the antiwar movement. In trying to decide whose side God favored in this war, we were shown with painful certitude that life is a more complicated mixture of good and evil than we earlier had assumed. King's own view on the immorality of the Vietnam experience, as expressed in *Danse Macabre*, corresponds precisely with such an interpretation:

> I was in college at the time, attending the University of Maine, and while I began college with political leanings too far to the right to actually become radicalized, by 1968 my mind had been changed forever about a number of fundamental questions....
>
> Now, I did not and do not believe that the hands of the Rockerfellers were utterly clean during that period, nor those of AT&T; I did and do believe that companies like Sikorsky and Douglas Aircraft and Dow Chemical and even the Bank of America subscribed more or less to the idea that war is good business.... In various ways throughout this book I've tried to suggest that the horror story is in many ways an optimistic, upbeat experience; that it is often the tough mind's way of coping with terrible problems which may not be supernatural at all but perfectly real. (296-8)

Burt and Vicky are therefore sacrificed because they are adult representatives of fallen, post-Vietnam America. Both have strayed from any sense of a belief in God, their marriage is in disharmony; both appear as selfish, stubborn, and unforgiving individuals; they are anxious to pass through Nebraska and travel on to "sunny, sinful California" (258); and Burt is a Vietnam veteran. References to this last point are made on three separate occasions, but the most significant citation occurs immediately after Burt becomes aware of the 1964 time setting. While standing on a sidewalk in the town, ironically expecting to discover "a school named after JFK" (260), the president who initiated American involvement in Vietnam, Burt smells fertilizer. The odor had always reminded him of his childhood in rural upstate New York, "but somehow this smell was different from the one he had grown up with.... There was a sickish sweet undertone. Almost a death smell. As a medical orderly in Vietnam, he had become well versed in that smell" (263). The association between Vietnam and Nebraska and its corn fields, and the disenchantment inherent in adult experience, is maintained on similar symbolic levels throughout the story. Nebraska and its corn are located in the "heartland" of America, its moral epicenter, and out of an effort to reestablish the purity and innocence of an earlier era, both the corn and the land itself seem to be demanding adult penance for a sin that originated in 1964.

King's corn god is furious with the adult world, demanding blood in exchange for reclaiming the land from its state of spiritual and physical barrenness. Burt discovers the god's maxim written on the cover of the town's registry: "Thus let the inquitous be cut down so that the ground may be fertile again saith the Lord God of Hosts" (267). The very fact that the ground needs to be made "fertile again" suggests that it has suffered from some kind of pestilence. And the "disease of the corn" in this tale, while ambiguous throughout, can be interpreted in terms of American defoliation of the Vietnamese landscape, as well as the more symbolic cultural "illness" or moral guilt and spiritual taint that accompanied American involvement in the conflict.

King's use of the corn deity undoubtedly owes its origins to anthropological studies of primitive cultures, where some variation of a corn god is often associated with the fertility of the land. To maintain the fecundity of the soil and to produce a bountiful harvest, these communities made frequent sacrifice in the spirit's honor. James Frazer dedicates an entire volume of the monumental work *The Golden Bough* to documenting these rituals. Various primitive societies conducted elaborate human sacrifices (and several of those still in existence continue the practice), usually to a corn-mother or a corn-maiden, in order to bless the forthcoming harvest. Among the plethora of illustrations Frazer cites, is this particularly relevant example from Mexico:

We have seen that the ancient Mexicans also sacrificed human beings at all the various stages in the growth of the maize, the age of the victims corresponding to the age of the corn; for they sacrificed new-born babes at sowing, older children when the grain had sprouted, and so on till it was fully ripe, when they sacrificed old men. No doubt the correspondence between the ages of the victims and the state of the corn was supposed to enhance the efficacy of the sacrifice. (Vol. 7, 237-8)

Jessie Weston's *From Ritual to Romance* further considers primitive man's sense of a connection between the status of his land and a deific presence. The legend of the Fisher King, a Christian precursor, emerged as an explanation for crop failure; the Fisher King's personal illness was reflected in the state of the country, which had become a wasteland. According to Weston, the Fisher King, who is a composite figure derived from a variety of fertility images including the more ancient corn god, "is not merely a deeply symbolic figure, but the essential centre . . . a being semi-divine, semi-human, standing between his people and the

land, and the unseen forces which control their destiny" (90).
Only through the great sacrifice of the Fisher King was it thought
possible to construct the basis for a future generation which would
make the wasteland fertile again.

The continuing series of human sacrifices commanded by
the corn god in "Children of the Corn" have been successful;
vitality has been restored to the American soil. The moral
wasteland that was the consequence of involvement in Vietnam
has been transformed into Nebraska corn growing in flawless
rows. Moreover, as Burt discovers while running wounded
through the open fields, the soil even contains a mysterious
recuperative power: "The ache in his arm had settled into a dull
throb that was nearly pleasant, and the good feeling was still
with him" (274). The corn diety has made the land, and all that
comes in contact with it, into a agrarian Arcadia, a neo-Eden
of pristine perfection and harmony. But to maintain this
environment, the corn deity exacts from this symbolic American
community in Nebraska a never-ending cycle of adult penance
and revenge. In fact, at the conclusion of the story the corn god
lowers the age of sacrifice from nineteen to eighteen, suggesting
that the inherited guilt and shame of Vietnam will never be
completely exorcised.

In *Danse Macabre*, King states that he has "purposely avoided
writing a novel with a 1960s time setting.... But those things
did happen: the hate, paranoia, and fear on both sides were all
too real" (158-9). King may not have directed his energies into
a full-length novel, but in "Children of the Corn" he has provided
us with a brief but frightening little allegory of the decade's
major historical event. Moreover, King makes his point by setting
many of his other stories and novels *just before* the eventful decade
of the Sixties. *The Body* is set in 1959; a portion of *It* shares
a 1958 reference frame; even Christine was a 1958 Plymouth.
Like George Eliot in *Adam Bede*, King often employs historical
backgrounds that are *on the eve of* some great upheaval in culture
and/or mores.

Perhaps just as significant as the historical setting for
"Children of the Corn," especially in light of its emphasis
throughout King's canon, is that the "adult world" represented
in this story is interpreted as sinful and in need of punishment.
In reaction to parental values deemed empty and materialistic,
the youth generation of the sixties celebrated its agelessness. "We
ain't never, never, gonna grow up," promised Yippie Jerry Rubin
in his pre-corporate finance days. "We're gonna be adolescents

forever!'' American youth were in the streets directing a cultural critique of their country's morality. Those who governed the nation—the adults—became the enemy; they had perpetuated the war in Vietnam and had sent America's children to perform the killing and the dying. Above all else, Vietnam was the sacrifice of the children, just as the trench warfare of World War I was; a needless sacrifice certainly—and even worse, an aimless one.

3

The theme of innocence betrayed is at the heart of "Children of the Corn." Indeed, this concept unifies the major work of King's canon: throughout his fiction, the power of evil to malign and pervert innocence is omnipresent. We have traced this tendency through a number of illustrations: Louis Creed and Jack Torrance sacrifice their families and sanities when they pursue the opposite extreme of innocence—represented by a working knowledge of the world's darkest mysteries and experiences. Most of the examples we have considered so far, however, have focused on adult misadventures—in government, societal institutions, personal morality. In "The Raft," King's retelling of the fall from grace is, in Michael Collings' words, a "rite of passage symbolizing loss of innocence" (146), and it is rendered from the child's point of view.

"The Raft" is narrowly centered around a late afternoon in the lives of four college students—two females and two males— poised on the very edge of adulthood. The significance of this transitional state to the story's meaning cannot be overemphasized. It is not only apparent in their ages and student status, but is likewise mirrored in the setting itself: "the end of the long Indian summer they had been enjoying.... Rachel said that summers had seemed to last forever when she was a girl, but now that she was an adult ('a doddering senile nineteen,' Deke joked, and she kicked his ankle), they get shorter every year" (246). Intoxicated on beer, determined to savor the last days of summer and their youth, all four swim out to a raft in the middle of a deserted Pennsylvania lake. Once on the raft, Randy, the story's principal character, notices an iridescent, circular object resembling an oil slick moving toward them. The object turns out to be alive—a gelatinous creature that eventually devours each of the students, one by one.

The monster is never clearly apprehended by any of the teenagers. Its vibrant array of incandescent colors works as a dangerous hallucinogen, entrapping the will of anyone who stares at it for too long. "It floated on the water, round and regular, like the top of a large steel drum, but the limber way it rode the swells made it clear that it was not the surface of a solid object" (249). In its ambiguity and destructive hunger, the dark circle (reminiscent of the spiral imagery in *Pet Sematary*) becomes a symbol of the mystery of adulthood—capable of mesmerizing at the same time as it plunders—and Randy in particular gains acute insight into this realm before he perishes.

Just before the deaths of Rachel and Deke, the first two to die, Randy becomes aware of the change taking place in them as a result of the terror they are encountering. Their apprehension is described in terms that suggest both a loss of innocence and a growing connection to adulthood. In watching Rachel standing on the edge of the raft moments before she is pulled into the water by the creature, Randy observes that beneath her "Sandy Duncan innocence," lurks a "neurotic prettiness" and a look in her eyes that could be interpreted as "free-floating anxiety" (252). Deke, the football star whose body "was as hard as Carrara marble" (259), likewise reveals his vulnerability when confronted with circumstances beyond his control: "Deke was sounding a little pissed off now, a little off-balance. A little scared? For the first time tonight, for the first time this month, this year, maybe for the first time in his whole life? Now there was an awesome thought—Deke loses his fear cherry" (257).

After Deke and Rachel are consumed in particularly graphic and grotesque fashions, La Verne and Randy make love; the act is not motivated by passion so much as stimulated by the need for human contact in the face of nature's cruelty. "The tactile sensations were incredible, fantastic. He was not experienced, but neither was he a virgin; he had made love with three girls and it had never been like this" (266). While engaged in intercourse, Randy's mind spirals back to a series of kaleidoscopic memories from adolescent summers—"the feel of summer, the texture; I can root for the Yankees from the bleachers, girls in bikinis on the beach...the Beach Boys oldies...firm breasts fragrant with Coppertone oil" (267)—until these memories are abruptly interrupted as La Verne is pulled from beneath him and into the water by a "twisting gruesome membrane" (267). The symbolism of this scene is apparent: Randy's first "real" sexual experience represents the bridge, as it is for most of us, between child and adult. The hydromonster, however, hideously severs Randy's ties to adolescence and thrusts him, naked and alone, into the adult world of pain and loss.

The creature's physical ambiguity helps to support its symbolic function as a living manifestation of the worst anxieties associated with adulthood. One by one his college friends, like his connections to adolescence, are stripped from Randy as he is forced into encountering the realities of adult life. Unlike the hopeful conclusion of "The Monkey," Randy's initiation into adulthood never invests him with any degree of control; the brutality merely intensifies and grows—like the monster itself after it consumes Rachel—until it literally overwhelms him. Stranded on the raft, surrounded by death and the encroaching cold of the autumn night, Randy discovers that his best friend and girl friend are lovers and have betrayed him; he realizes that the bliss of sexuality is only a momentary reprieve from the terrors of the dark; and most of all, in his last hours of life, bereft of human comfort and anticipating his own demise, Randy learns what we all must in the face of adult perimeters—that the cocoon of adolescence, symbolized appropriately in the warm recollections of summers past, is no longer retrievable once we have emerged from it.

4

In Stephen King's landscape, the failure of love and understanding triggers disaster. Evil is perpetuated through legacies of sin, based in social, cultural, mythical, and historical contexts, and handed down from one generation to the next. Adulthood, because of its litany of selfish mistakes, broken promises, cruel machinations, and drunken excesses, fully embodies this legacy of human corruption; adults show themselves capable of betrayal at any point. The inevitable violence and cruelty which are the usual end results of adult values and behavior force many of King's adolescent protagonists to relinquish their tentative hold on innocence and sensitivity.

In the short story "Last Rung on the Ladder," an attorney becomes so involved with his career and his reputation in the world that he fails to heed his misdirected younger sister's plea for help. As a child, he was always there to protect her and lend his support, but as an adult he is too preoccupied. When she finally commits suicide, in large measure because of his failure to become involved, he is left with an enormous burden of guilt.

The novella *Apt Pupil*, from the collection *Different Seasons*, works from a similar set of suppositions. Todd Bowden, a precocious adolescent fascinated with the grisly details of Nazi Germany, discovers an aging war criminal, Dussander, hiding in his suburban American neighborhood. Todd's attraction to the atrocities that occurred under Dussander's command are initially based on an innocent curiosity: the urge to discover, "with a mixture of revulsion and excitement" (115), what took place inside the concentration camps. In fact, Dussander is absolutely perplexed when he learns that the child has no intension of extorting money from him: "He stared at Dussander with an open and appealing frankness. 'Why...I want to hear about it. That's all. That's all I want. Really' " (124).

As Todd practices more devious and intricate methods of extracting a personal history from the former Nazi officer, their interaction brings Dussander back into intimate contact with his past. "He had been forced to give up a part of himself. Now he had reclaimed it" (155). Reliving his moral misconduct during the war affects his new life in California, as he is compelled to commit a series of murders in his kitchen. Moreover, through his daily contacts with the boy, Dussander "tends a small but perfect flame of hatred deep in [Todd's] heart" (245). Over a period of years, this flame enlarges into a conflagration. As a direct consequence of his involvement with the Nazi, Todd's interest in sports and schoolwork is abandoned in favor of stalking and butchering helpless drunks and street people; his emerging sexuality is stimulated only by perverse fantasies of women in bondage, forced to suffer sadistic violations; his sense of personal morality is sacrificed as he doctors his failing report card grades; and his relationship with his parents, formerly characterized by a playful intimacy, is now clouded by Todd's need to sustain elaborate barriers between the vicious self he is becoming and their image of the innocent child he had been.

Some of King's best creative fiction can be found in the first two-thirds of this novella (the last third introduces too many new characters and coincidences so that the book's intensity of focus is severely weakened), as he methodically takes us through a study of negative adult influence and the corrupting fusion of evil. These elements are most effectively handled, especially in the descriptions of the slow metamorphosis taking place in Todd. Early in the book, Todd has several dreams about the world Dussander has been describing, "but it was nothing he couldn't handle" (131). As his obsession with the Nazi deepens, however, Todd's dreams become more vivid, less malleable. His dreams are like the successive stages of embryonic development in a chrysalis, signalling Todd's transformation—from the dissolution of the all-conference, all-American child, to the emergence of the corrupt adult who has lost sight of all moral principles. As Dussander informs him, " 'Seven hundred thousand died at Patin. To the world at large I am a criminal, a monster, even the butcher your scandal-rags would have me. You are an accessory to all that, my boy' "(161).

Following several months of exposure to Dussander, Todd has another dream, as well as his first nocturnal emission, and this dream sequence, like the short story "The Raft," employs sexual initiation as a symbol of the child's emergence into the brutality characteristic of King's adult world. Todd finds himself in front of a half-naked Dussander and a young Jewish girl, the latter bound to the four corners of an examination table. Dussander directs him to secure a hollow dildo over his small, erect penis, which he then uses to penetrate the young woman. In this sadomasochistic fantasy, Todd becomes a literal "appendage" of the Nazi, discovering pleasure in another person's pain. And as Todd rapes this defenseless woman, Dussander is symbolically raping Todd, recording "pulse, blood pressure, respiration, alpha waves, beta waves, stroke count" (189). The dream fully illustrates the price Todd pays for the betrayal of his innocence; he chooses to become a living extension of history, violating the secrets of the past so thoroughly that they erupt into the present. Indeed, near the conclusion of the book, Dussander asks Todd to drink with him in celebration of the student's improved grades. The scene is easily overlooked, but its significance is greater than the Nazi's ostensible toast. The bourbon Todd consumes is symbolic of the corruption inherent in King's adult world, a realm in which Dussander serves as high priest. The jelly-glass Todd uses to drink the whiskey, of course, represents the childhood from which he has forever broken:

Dussander got up. He went to one of the kitchen cabinets and took down a small glass. This glass had once held jelly. Cartoon characters danced around the rim. Todd recognized them all—Fred and Wilma Flintstone, Barney and Betty Rubble, Pebbles and Bamm-Bamm. He had grown up with them. He watched as Dussander wiped this jelly-glass almost ceremonially with a dishtowel. He watched as Dussander set it in front of him. He watched as Dussander poured a finger of bourbon into it.

"What's that for?" Todd muttered. "I don't drink. Drinking's for cheap stewbums like you."

"Lift your glass, boy. It is a special occasion. Today you drink."

Todd looked at him for a long moment, then picked up the glass. Dussander clicked his cheap ceramic cup smartly against it. (196)

As the novella progresses, Todd comes to identify fully with Nazi dogma. He begins to categorize and manipulate people to his own advantage. Paralleling his affiliation with a Nazi world-view, the boy's increasing need to commission his own acts of brutality appears further justifiable when he interprets them in light of his own culture's adult values and rationalizations:

> He supposed he might have to kill again, and maybe more than once. It was too bad, but of course their time of usefulness as human creatures was over. Except their usefulness to Todd, of course. And Todd, like everyone else he knew, was only tailoring his lifestyle to fit his own particular needs as he grew older. Really, he was no different than anybody. You had to make your own way in the world; if you were going to get along, you had to do it by yourself. (213)

Todd Bowden may never have been a paragon of moral purity or innocence; in fact, his psychological torment of the Nazi from the very beginning suggests quite the opposite. But steady contact with Dussander pushes him into a deeper, more serious, and personal participation in evil. As psychological studies of exposure to aggressive acts indicate, the more an individual is exposed to violence, the greater his response to it. Todd's prurient interest in the adult knowledge Dussander possesses becomes addictive; the simple curiosity that initiated their relationship—"all the gooshy stuff" (124)—evolves into an active presence neither man can finally control. *Apt Pupil* once again suggests the depravity King sees as indicative of adult experience. The novella more than illustrates the danger inherent in Richard Bowden's naive assumption that " 'for a kid the whole world's a laboratory...and he'll be all the stronger for having knocked around a few corners' " (132). His son, Todd Bowden, enters the "world's laboratory" as an apt pupil; the monster that emerges two years later owes its creation to the particular course of study it discovers there.

5

King's children, like those found in Dickens' novels, illustrate the failings and abuses of adult society. The destruction of their innocence accomplishes more than a simple restating of the universal theme of the fall from grace; it enlarges to include a specific critique of respective societies and cultures as well. As I have argued elsewhere in this text, King's fiction works from the premise of a fallen, corrupted mortal world. This tragic vision is provided its clearest dramatization when King probes the dark realities of adult life as they are perceived by children. Many of his adolescents—like Todd Bowden and the children of the corn—are victimized by the influence of adult culpability and sin. These young people are made to sacrifice their innocence when they inherit the moral mistakes of an older generation. In making the transition into adulthood, their knowledge of the world is shaped by painful tragedy, and often culminates in their own deaths. As Todd Bowden realizes shortly before commencing his own personal holocaust, the American adult landscape is composed of treacherous terrain, where even the most intense light cannot penetrate all the shadows: "It was as if, in the bright and careful arrangement he had made, in that a-place-for-everything-and-everything-in-its-place kitchen of his mind, a dark and bloody intruder now lurched and shambled, looking for a place to die" (215).

In *Danse Macabre*, King asserts that "if the horror story is our rehearsal for death, then its strict moralities make it also a reaffirmation of life and good will and simple imagination— just one more pipeline to the infinite" (380). Although to this point this study has provided confirmation of the "strict moralities" operating in King's fictional microcosm more than those elements of reaffirmation, I do not mean to suggest that King writes only about themes of annihilation and spiritual futility. There are, in fact, several major protagonists whose "reaffirmation of life and good will" enables them to triumph over the particular horrors they encounter. The final two chapters of this book focus on the conflict between symbols of human corruption (represented in King's portrayal of social and cultural institutions) and the individual's struggle to avoid its entrapments. Those characters who manage to circumvent such enslavement—several of his adolescent protagonists and a handful of adults who maintain child-like loyalties and a romantic faith in life—are the only true survivors in King's canon. Emerging from their moral voyage into worldly evil with their independence intact, they summon an inner strength that is greater than the forces of destruction, both human and supernatural, that surround them.

Chapter 6
In Flight to Freedom:
The Voyage to Selfhood
and Survival

Early in *The Stand*, Larry Underwood is forced to traverse the entire length of the Lincoln Tunnel on foot. Most of his journey is in darkness, punctuated only by the sounds of rats feasting amongst the decaying dead and his own frightened footsteps. In the novella *The Body* from the collection *Different Seasons*, Gordie Lachance must walk along a narrow train trestle high above a shallow stream. "If a train came, it was maybe enough room to avoid getting plastered...but the wind generated by the highballing freight would surely sweep you off to fall to a certain death against the rocks just below the surface of the shallow running water" (366). And in *The Talisman*, Jack Sawyer must pass through the Oakley Tunnel in upstate New York, an experience that leaves him nearly claustrophobic.

The image of the tunnel or narrow passageway is used in each of these instances to highlight the anxieties of the characters who must pass through it. In each case, however, the successful completion of these "night journeys," to borrow Douglas Winter's phrase, also symbolizes the emergence of a new stage in the development of the individual involved. For Larry Underwood, the Lincoln's Tunnel's enclosure parallels his self-enclosed past as a rock star in the pre-plague world. His emergence into the light at the other side of the tunnel is an image of rebirth signalling the inception of a new, more responsible personality. The passageways that Jack Sawyer and Gordie Lachance endure mark transition phases in their life-journeys as well. The Oakley Tunnel in *The Talisman* and the train trestle in *The Body* enlarge into symbols of the social landscape that dominates both books: like the trestle and tunnel, the societies Jack and Gordie encounter on their respective voyage-quests are delineated best in terms of violent constriction; the adult world and its institutions seek to entrap and exploit both boys—and when this fails, to kill them. Their survival occurs only because of their resolute commitment to resist these suffocating forces. Throughout King's work, his characters are made to walk through dark corridors similar to the ones just described. King acknowledges the importance of these symbolic voyages through the seasoned reflections of his autobiographical narrator, Gordie Lachance, who years later realizes that "the rite of passage *is* a magic corridor and so we always provide an aisle—it's what you walk down when you get married, what they carry you down when you get buried. Our corridor was those twin rails, and we walked between them" (415). Those protagonists who summon the inner strength to endure the fear they encounter within these circumscribed conditions usually emerge with a greater degree of independence and moral resolve. It is as if their voyage has brought them into direct contact with their own deepest fears; and in passing through them, each character is endowed with a new level of self-control and confidence.

The attribute of self-control is the predominant feature that distinguishes the writer's moral heroes and heroines from the amoral or immoral corruption of his social and bestial worlds. In *Danse Macabre*, King argues that an honest and accurate perception of morality cannot be measured in decrepit social institutions, by conforming to the "bottomless conservatism" of white suburban America (169). Rather, one must look to

where it has always [existed]: in the hearts and minds of men and women of good will. In the case of the writer, this may mean relearning old lessons of human values and human conduct.... The horror writer [is] not just [a] writer but [a] human being, mortal man or woman, just another passenger in the boat, another pilgrim on the way to whatever there is. And we hope that if he sees another pilgrim fall down that he will write about it—but not before he or she has helped the fallen one to his or her feet, brushed off his or her clothes, and seen if he or she is all right, and able to go on. If such behavior is to be, it cannot be as a result of an intellectual moral stance; it is because there is such a thing as love, merely a practical fact, a practical force in human affairs. (374-5)

The moral survivors of King's fiction are those individuals who extricate themselves from the ethical morass of mainstream America's adult value system, while at the same time adhering to the tenet that "there is such a thing as love." In the majority of his books, King is essentially retelling the story of Mark Twain's

Huckleberry Finn: that in order to endure morally, the individual must balance a love for his fellow man with a resolve to avoid his decadent societal institutions. Throughout King's fiction, only those characters who follow Huck's rebellious example by continually "lighting out for the territory ahead of the rest" emerge with their independence intact and a set of inviolable ethical principles.

1

In their two-way odyssey to view the remains of a young boy killed by a train, the four children in King's novella *The Body* are as much in flight from their homes and community as they are curious about seeing Ray Brower's corpse. Each of the four adolescent protagonists in this book has been severely abused or neglected. Vern Tesso lives in absolute terror of his older brother, and his parents appear unwilling and unable to save him from daily beatings. Teddy Duchamp's ears have been horribly mutilated, the result of his father's pressing his head against the side of a woodstove. Moreover, his father's insanity has given rise to Teddy's own psychological maladjustments: the child is obsessed with taking risks that endanger his life— dodging trucks and trains at the very last possible moment. Chris Chambers "didn't talk much about his dad, but we all knew he hated him like poison. Chris was marked up every two weeks or so, bruises on his cheeks and neck or one eye swelled up and as colorful as a sunset" (315-6). And while the story's young narrator, Gordie Lachance, has never been physically abused by his parents, his attitude toward adulthood is just as negative. In his eyes, his parents always favored his older brother, Dennis, and when the latter dies, their response is to withdraw even further from Gordie: "I did a book report in high school on this novel called *The Invisible Man*. . . . This *Invisible Man* is about a Negro. Nobody ever notices him at all unless he fucks up. People look right through him. When he talks, nobody answers. He's like a black ghost. Once I got it, I ate that book up like it was a John D. MacDonald, because that cat Ralph Ellison was writing about *me*" (320).

Against this backdrop of familial violence and broken relationships, the four boys are united, at least in their sympathy for one another's plight. In their journey to view Ray Brower's dead body, however, the children are unaware that they are really travelling toward their own destiny; by the end of the story, three of the four have died violent deaths. And the fourth, the tale's narrator, is left years later with the realization that his memory of Brower's decaying body is still inextricably tied to his own life:

> I've thought of driving to the end of the Black Harlow Road in my almost new Ford van and getting out of it some bright summer morning, all by myself, my wife and children far off in another world where, if you turn a switch, lights come on in the dark.... It usually comes early in the morning, when my wife is showering and the kids are watching *Batman* and *Scooby-Doo* on channel 38 out of Boston, and I am feeling the most like the pre-adolescent Gordie Lachance that once strode the earth, walking and talking and occasionally crawling on his belly like a reptile. That boy was *me*, I think. And the thought which follows, chilling me like a dash of cold water, is: *Which boy do you mean?* (436)

The journey these children undertake leads them through the befouled depths of twentieth-century America, past garbage dumps and polluted rivers that resemble the ashheaps in Fitzgerald's *The Great Gatsby*: a wasteland reflecting the moral values of the society which produced it. The four boys engage in a desperate struggle against death, even as they are searching for its handiwork. Traveling through this valley of corruption, the boys are, in a basic sense, traveling through an inferno of the Damned. In the Castle Rock wasteland, it is people like Ace and his gang, "consumers" in the most appalling sense of the word, who survive: feeding upon the weaknesses, the genuine emotions, or the fears of other human beings, they move like profane machines of flesh, using and breaking, and discarding all that gets in their path. Indeed, destructive images of the machine age represent a central motif in the book and are always employed as a threat to the boys' welfare: the train itself, thundering along without regard for young legs that stumble across its tracks; Milo and his dog from hell, Chopper, who patrol the junkyard of America, "filled with all the American things that get empty, wear out, or just don't work anymore" (345); the machine-like personalities of the Castle Rock adults, who are always prepared to inflict damage with poundings from their fists; and the mill town environment itself, a destiny that appears almost mechanically prearranged as it waits to shape these children into its own image and likeness.

The journey-quest of the children, as is often the case in King's fiction, becomes a symbolic voyage into a psychic landscape with profound moral implications. Teddy and Vern reject the opportunity to break from the codes and values of their society when they abandon Chris and Gordie in their confrontation with Ace and his gang of street punks. Ray Brower's corpse parallels Teddy and Vern's own moral "deaths," for upon returning from this journey they proceed to follow in the bloody footsteps of the older boys and their Castle Rock parents: "When the casts came off and the bruises healed, Vern and Teddy just drifted away. They had discovered a whole new group of contemporaries that they could lord it over. Most of them were real wets—scabby, scrubby little fifth-grade assholes—but Vern and Teddy kept bringing them to the treehouse, ordering them around, strutting like Nazi generals" (446).

In contrast, Chris and Gordie use the journey as a rite of passage that completely severs their already tenuous connection to Castle Rock values. In their confrontation with Ace and the older boys over ownership of Brower's corpse, the two boys declare their independence from the adult world's tyrannical premise that the weak must always remain subordinate to the strong. Although they are severely beaten for their rebellion, this decision inspires Chris and Gordie to develop their bond of friendship until it becomes an alternative to the sterility of their families and the larger corruption of their community.

> We both dated through high school, but no girl ever came between us. Does that sound like we went faggot? It would have to most of our old friends, Vern and Teddy included. But it was only survival. We were clinging to each other in deep water. I've explained about Chris, I think; my reasons for clinging to him were less definable. His desire to get away from Castle Rock and out of the mill's shadow seemed to me to be my best part, and I could not just leave him to sink or swim on his own. If he had drowned, that part of me would have drowned with him, I think. (449-450)

Chris and Gordie maintain a place at the center of King's moral scheme because of their unflinching commitment to one another in the face of individuals and circumstances seeking to ensnare them. Gordie's successful job of tutoring Chris so that both could attend college is an unselfish act that, at least momentarily, allows the boys to disassociate themselves from the same cycle of violence that restricts all the other social interactions in this book.

> Chris enrolled in the college courses in his second year of junior high— he and I both knew that if he waited any longer it would be too late; he would never catch up. Everyone jawed at him about it: his parents, who thought he was putting on airs, his friends, most of whom dismissed him

as a pussy, the guidance counsellor, who didn't believe he could do the work, and most of all the teachers, who didn't approve of this duck-tailed, leather-jacketed, engineer-booted apparition who had materialized without warning in their classrooms. (448)

The journey to ethical alternatives is initiated by Gordie and Chris in their literal voyage to "discover" the dead child. For them, Ray Brower's mutilated corpse comes to symbolize the dead worlds of adult society and, more specifically, Castle Rock's morality. Their homes and community are emblematic of the type of social environment that often destroys King's protagonists, indeed that eventually swallows Vern and Teddy: a senseless arrangement of vulgar appetites in which motion has replaced direction, impulse has replaced moral choice, and love has been reduced to a process of mutual cannibalism. The story of Gordie and Chris's relationship, however, is the story of wonder and devotion pitted against the machine of society's false values; this machine, so clearly represented by the actions of the unseen parents in this novella, first spawns and then devours its own progeny, existing for no other purpose than its own digestion. In their efforts to avoid inclusion in this mechanistic world, the two boys construct a miniature society based upon the radical values of individual courage and interpersonal loyalty and respect. As Chris informs Gordie, certainly echoing King's own sentiments, " 'Kids lose *everything* unless somebody looks out for them and if your folks are too fucked up to do it then maybe I ought to' " (393).

2

Midway through *The Stand*, sociologist Glen Bateman, in a conversation with Stu Redman, speculates on the origins of human society and what occurs to men and women as this interaction enlarges:

Shall I tell you what sociology teaches us about the human race? I'll give it to you in a nutshell. Show me a man or woman alone and I'll show you a saint. Give me two and they'll fall in love. Give me three and they'll invent that charming thing we call "society." Give me four and they'll build a pyramid. Give me five and they'll make one an outcast. Give me six and they'll reinvent prejudice. Give me seven and in seven years they'll reinvent warfare. Man may have been made in the image of God, but human society was made in the image of His opposite number, and is always trying to get back home. (253)

This un-illusioned attitude toward the evolution of organized society can be traced throughout King's fiction; Bateman may be his most articulate and convincing spokesperson on this subject, but the predominant theme of negativism that King associates with human sociability is plainly restated in nearly every one of his books. Arguing a thesis closely aligned to Rousseau's in *The Social Contract*, King clearly believes that we are born "noble savages," but as we enter into ever-expanding social contracts, whatever our degree of inherent nobility weakens into corruption. As we have seen in his examples of adolescent despoilation, the more extensive the social contact, the greater the potential for acts of evil. The converse of this thesis, of course, is that the individual can maintain his or her moral freedom and human dignity only as long as he or she remains an individual. For Glen Bateman, and likewise for his creator, once a social relationship enlarges beyond two people, the dangers attendant to conformity and depersonalization become immediate—and grow progressively stronger with each step toward transforming a social microcosm into a macrocosm.

Following Bateman's sobering premise—indeed, it resonates through Stu Redman's mind—two of King's most heroic and persuasive protagonists, Redman and Frannie Goldsmith in *The Stand*, elect to leave the world's only remaining human community they helped to establish in Colorado. Their journey back to Maine is not merely informed by a sentimental nostalgia to return to Frannie's birthplace in order to raise their own children. More important, they are motivated by an increasing fear that the Boulder community is becoming a mirror of the society that existed prior to the superflu:

> It wouldn't be such a bad thing, Stu thought, watching Fran pump water, if the Free Zone did fall apart. Glen Bateman would think so, he was quite sure. Its purpose has been served, Glen would say. Best to disband before—
>
> Before what?...
>
> What happens after you give guns to the deputies? he asked himself. What's the logical progression? And it seemed that it was the scholarly, slightly dry voice of Glen Bateman that spoke in answer. You give them bigger guns. And police cars. And when you discover a Free Zone community down in Chile or maybe up in Canada, you make Hugh Petrella the Minister of Defense just in case, and maybe you start sending out search parties, because after all—....
>
> As he followed her inside Mother Abagail's house he thought it would be better, much better, if they did break down and spread. Postpone organization as long as possible. It was organization that always seemed

to cause the problem. You didn't have to give the cops guns until the cops couldn't remember the names...the faces... (815-6)

Like Frannie and Stu, there are a number of characters in King's fiction who discover society's threat to their individuality and moral stability. In the novel *Carrie*, the only person who provides Carrie with an element of sincere compassion is Sue Snell. The motivations behind her response are complicated but explicit: Sue is aware that joining her classmates in their locker room torment of Carrie is a violation of her own ethical principles. But equally significant is Snell's dramatic enlargement of this event toward the realization that society shapes individuals into patterns of collective behavior, regardless of how morally repugnant that behavior becomes. Consequently, her kindness to Carrie is really an act of social rebellion; by treating Carrie humanely, she hopes to save herself from a future of unconscionable conformity:

And having something she had always longed for—a sense of place, of security, of status—she found that it carried uneasiness with it like a darker sister. It was not the way she had conceived it. There were dark things lurking around her warm circle of light.... The word she was avoiding was expressed *To Conform*, in the infinitive, and it conjured miserable images of hair rollers, long afternoons in front of the ironing board in front of the soap operas while hubby was off busting heavies in an anonymous Office...of fighting with desperate decorum to keep the niggers out of Kleen Korners, armed with signs and petitions and sweet, slightly desperate smiles.
Carrie, it was that goddamned Carrie, that was her fault. Perhaps before today she had heard distant, circling footfalls around her lighted place, but tonight, hearing her own sordid, crummy story, she saw the actual silhouettes of all these things, and yellow eyes that glowed like flashlights in the dark. (45-6)

In choosing to reject the corrupt machinery of society—its unwholesome organizations and authority—King's characters become pariahs, left to discover new meanings for themselves. Like Twain's vision of Huck and Jim alone on the Mississippi River, King's fiction appears to suggest that psychologically balanced lives are possible only in small, interpersonal relationships which subsist outside the domination of existing American social institutions and adult value codes.

While this thesis may appear scandalously "un-American," as it emerges in response to the failure of our cultural institutions, it more closely reflects a fervent, prototypically American belief in starting over—shucking the past and inventing the future.

Unlike the European, who for better and for worse, maintains close ties to his cultural roots and traditions, the American has always prided himself on being able to declare that he is something quite different from what his parents were—and, as a corollary, from what the rest of his society is. From the early Puritan diaries, to Emerson's essays, to King's fiction, Americans have always perceived themselves as citizens of a new world. Asians and Europeans view this national consciousness with a mixture of awe and contempt, but in striving to "make it new," our literature has always mirrored the American's urge to renew himself—and it is difficult to feel either contemptuous or despairing about any movement that promises survival, if not salvation, within the process of change.

3

In King's novella *Cycle of the Werewolf*, the werewolf, a creature typically associated with the male gender, manifests the same helpless rage, frustration, and viciousness that delineates the adult masculine world elsewhere in King's canon. The werewolf appears only once a month on nights of a full moon. This suggests a parallel to a woman's menstruation cycle: If, during her menstrual period, a female is more acutely aware of her biological rhythms as an element distinguishing her femininity, the werewolf's cycle of bestial transformation reconfirms King's attitude toward the adult male's innate viciousness and propensity for capricious violence. Moreover, the werewolf grows massive amounts of hair; its muscles become more powerful and hyperextended; in short, in its transmogrified condition the human world revels in its link to the animal realm, satisfying a blood hunger through acts of brutality against other living beings.

The town of Tarker's Mills lives in fear of this creature yet, like the citizens of Jerusalem's Lot in the novel *'Salem's Lot*, is reluctant to take action against it. Somewhere in their collective unconsciousness the people of Tarker's Mills sense that whatever is responsible for causing such carnage in the town is a member of their human community. "The town," King informs us, "keeps its secrets" (29). Also, the fact that the beast is a Baptist minister during daylight hours further strengthens the creature's connection to the community it ravages by night. The werewolf is viewed as a passing phenomenon that is either not as dangerous as suspected, or a problem that will eventually take care of itself. Only the werewolf himself, Reverend Lester Lowe, comprehends the full universality of the beast's affiliation with the human world. As his dream vividly illustrates, the werewolf is merely an extension of social man, his propensity for sin finally acknowledged without veneer:

> The Beast, he tells them, is everywhere. The Great Satan, he tells them, can be anywhere. At a high school dance. Buying a deck of Marlboros and a Bic butane lighter down at the Trading Post. Standing in front of Brighton's Drug, eating a Slim Jim,...Watch for the Beast, for he may smile and say he is your neighbor, but oh my brethren, his teeth are sharp and you may mark the uneasy way in which his eyes roll. He is the Beast, and he is here, now, in Tarker's Mills. He—
>
> But here he breaks off, his eloquence gone, because something terrible is happening out there in his sunny church. His congregation is beginning to change, and he realizes with horror that they are turning into werewolfs, all of them, all three hundred of them. (45-6)

Young Marty Coslaw is the only member of Tarker's Mills who can or is willing to confront the werewolf. Outside the adult community by virtue of his being both a child and a cripple, Marty's parents view him as a difficult problem; even their most mundane interactions are painful reminders of Marty's difference: "The truth is, Marty makes Herman Coslaw a little nervous. Herman lives in a world of violently active children, kids who run races, bash baseballs, swim rally sprints. And in the midst of directing all this he would sometimes look up and see Marty, somewhere close by, sitting in his wheelchair, watching" (61).

Isolated and quietly tormented by a society that cannot comprehend his affliction and, as a consequence, will never totally accept him, Marty turns to his only ally, another outsider, Uncle Al. Al neither pities Marty nor treats him condescendingly; he simply responds to the boy with genuine and spontaneous affection. Perhaps he identifies with Marty's isolation, as Al is an eccentric, single, middle-aged man with no intention of conforming to adult mores. Marty and Al, like Chris and Gordie in *The Body*, adhere to values that contrast sharply with those represented elsewhere in the community. It is because of their mutual respect for one another, coupled with their acceptance of myth and supernatural phenomena, that they are finally able to destroy the evil represented by the werewolf. Unlike those in the community who immediately discredit Marty's claim that he encountered the beast one night on his front lawn, Al believes enough of the boy's story to produce the two silver bullets that will eventually be used to kill the monster.

4

Marty and Al actively confront the existence of the werewolf and successfully dispose of him because, unlike the other humans in Tarker's Mills, they are not rendered helpless by a recognition of their own evil in the werewolf's. Moreover, in this instance child and adult work in harmony to save each other. United by the differences that separate them from the rest of society, Marty and Al endure because of their shared responsibilities for one another. In King's fiction, physical and moral survival most often occur as the result of a union between adults who have not lost their respect for children, and children who have come to trust these adults primarily because they have no where else to turn.

Relationships similar to Al and Marty's reappear in much more elaborate forms elsewhere in King's canon. In *The Shining*, *The Stand*, and *The Talisman*, King's vulnerable heroes and heroines are aided by older black adults who possess the gift of prophecy, a highly developed sense of moral integrity, and an instinctive understanding of how the world operates. Moreover, the latter sustain a code of ethics that is foreign to values King presents in his descriptions of mainstream America. They are outcasts from this society, representing the aged, the poor, and the non-white. As such, King's blacks are in the position of instructing and guiding his younger, highly impressionable, white protagonists through the respective wastelands of each novel and toward a vision of greater self-perception and moral growth.

Speedy Parker in *The Talisman*, works as a caretaker for an old amusement park and is considered little more than a drunken bum. Yet he is the only person in this book who offers Jack Sawyer the assistance necessary for survival. Speedy instructs Jack about the Territories, encourages him throughout his difficult quest, and helps Sawyer develop an acute ability to exercise his own ethical judgment. The black man is more than Jack's friend; he is a teacher and a moral guardian: "Speedy's instructions were the only schooling he was getting, but that made him feel better" (11). Jack and Speedy share a bond because neither the black outcast nor the adolescent outsider occupies a secure place in American society. Their relationship challenges the core limitations of this society, and therefore must remain secretive and illicit.

The Talisman, like so many of the tales examined in this book, is not merely a *buldungsroman*, or novel of maturation, but also a story about the corruption of American society and values. Bernadette Bosky cites Straub's own analysis of the narrative in her essay "Stephen King and Peter Straub: Fear and Friendship": "What Steve [King] describes as 'Reagan's America' is almost implicit in the elements we assembled for the book. The book does seem to be about the death of the land, the terrible poisoning of the land" (70). Jack's mother, queen of the B-rated movies, and Laura De Loessian, queen of the Territories, appear to be dying for similar reasons: their illnesses, like the affliction of the Fisher King in Eliot's *The Waste Land*, are symptomatic of the spiritual condition in their respective countries. Indeed, it is clear enough that the novel's center of evil, Morgan Sloat, represents the business ethics of modern American capitalism pursued to their extreme:

> Uncle Morgan lived for business, for deal-making and hustling; and he was so ambitious that he challenged every even faintly dubious call in a tennis match, so ambitious in fact that he cheated in the penny-ante card games his son had now and then coaxed him into joining. At least, Jack *thought* that Uncle Morgan had been cheating in a couple of their games...not a man who thought that defeat demanded graciousness. (30)

Sloat's reign of terror—both in the boardrooms of America and on the clay highways of the Territories—is the controlling image for most of the experiences Jack undergoes in the course of his journey. From Smokey Updike's dark cynicism to Sunlight Gardener's sadistic penances, the America portrayed in this novel is a land of unbridled ambition and consummate greed that bears great similarities to the Poland described in Jerzy Kosinski's own tale of adolescent horror *The Painted Bird*. As Jack gains travelling experience, he comes to realize that he can trust very few people, that there exists a highly sophisticated web of communication linking Morgan Sloat to most of the strangers with whom Jack must interact in both worlds. Sawyer, like the Huck Finn prototype on whom he was modelled, must flee continually from violence and deceit; with the exceptions of his friend Wolf and Speedy himself, every human being and social institution Jack encounters on his voyage to California seeks to enslave him physically or manipulate him psychologically.

Since they remain extrinsic to the corruption and greed characteristic of King's modern America, Jack and Speedy are free to express their love and dedication for each other. So deep is their commitment that the young boy becomes a virtual extension of the older man: "He did not understand why, but Speedy seemed to be able to communicate emotion directly to him: as if they had not met just a week before, but years ago, and had shared far more than a few words in a deserted arcade" (31). Just as Twain's Huckleberry Finn learns to accept humility and the burden of human responsibility from his black friend and mentor Jim, Speedy is Jack Sawyer's guide and guardian throughout *The Talisman*; his inspiration, wisdom, gifts, and near-mystical presence help Jack to endure his trials and to emerge from them with a degree of courage and moral self-confidence that rivals Twain's young protagonist. On the river, at home with nature and free to indulge an appreciation for the primitive, Twain's Huck and Jim discover a sanctuary from the evils of nineteenth-century civilization. Speedy and Jack's uncomplicated union also poses a clear alternative to the bleak and sterile social landscape of contemporary America as well as the mythological Territories.

In the course of the novel, Jack's commitment to Speedy enlarges to include the friendly werewolf, Wolf. The werewolf is, in at least this capacity, an extension of Speedy himself. As Jack's contact with greater levels of social corruption grow, his connection to the primitive world, represented on an imaginary continuum from Speedy to Wolf at the extreme, expands accordingly. The simple mysteries celebrated by, and manifested within, primitive life, the greatest of which is love, is antithetical to civilization's great sophistries and betrayals. The werewolf's intrinsic lament for America's polluted world is meant to contrast with Morgan Sloat's sophisticated design to defile the landscape even further. Wolf's capacity for love connects him to Jack and Speedy in a triangle that celebrates life; but Speedy and Jack are likewise tied to Wolf as well: all three are lost and out of place in a world that will never be home. Their survival is possible only because of their dedication to one another in the face of civilization's barbarism. Wolf does not harm Jack during the former's night of full moon carnage because he continually adheres to the principle of "never harming the herd," even during the werewolf's moment of deepest blood lust.

King and Straub have written a book that reflects some of the major recurring themes found in nineteenth and twentieth century American literature. Jack's journey across the landscape of America is a voyage from innocence to experience. The Jack Sawyer we leave at the conclusion of *The Talisman*—riding the train bravely through the Blasted Lands and inspiring the terrified Richard Sloat with his self-confidence—bears little resemblence to the child who emerges from the Oatley Tunnel clinging to his toothbrush and memories of a more secure life with his mother. Jack gains a faith in himself and his own individuality at the same time as he learns that this selfhood is always threatened by social institutions and its various entrapments.

Throughout American literature there are a myriad of comparisons relevant to this theme, from *Huckleberry Finn* to Hemingway's Nick Adams stories to *Catcher in the Rye*. Moreover, in the act of eschewing civilized virtues, many of the protagonists in American literature parallel Jack's acceptance of the primitive. In Melville's *Moby Dick*, for example, Ishmael learns that Queequeg is no force of evil or maliciousness; in fact, he is quite the opposite. In associating with the tattooed pagan, Ishmael finds an answer to the spiritual void of his own empty Calvinist faith and personal alienation from shore society. Queequeg opens him to accept a multidimensional world that extends from man to whale and then to God. The savage's simple example of unselfish love is a reminder to Ishmael of what is hopeful and life-affirming, and thus serves as an effective counterpoint to the sterile precepts of Father Mapple and the one dimensionality of Ahab's obsession.

Ishmael and Queequeg, Huck and Jim, Natty Bumppo and Chingachgook, all these relationships exist outside the acceptable boundaries of American social life. As Leslie Fiedler has detailed in *Love and Death in the American Novel*, these unions are established between the young, often naive white male, and the dark stranger whose roots are pagan and primitive. Each of these white males comes eventually to identify with the sweet vitality that lurks just beneath the repulsive and terrifying exteriors of their savage mentors. Most often this identification helps the young protagonist to appreciate not only the dangers inherent in organized society, but the larger beauty of the untamed natural environment. These unions help the white characters to recapture the primordial vision of America as a neo-Eden, of nature's spirituality in contrast to the corruption of human society. Queequeg's representation of an intrinsic humanity beneath his evil physical appearance parallels Ishmael's education that at the symbolic center of the monster whale is not Ahab's viciousness, but the exotic beauty of whale sperm (Chapter 94) and ambergris (Chapter 92). Similarly, Wolf's appreciation for the Territories is a reminder of the world America once was before it was spoiled by the business ethics of modern capitalism. Like Huckleberry Finn in the company of Jim on the river or Ishmael with Queequeg floating among the nurturing whales on a placid ocean in The Grand Armada (Chapter 87), Sawyer's sensitivities are heightened by his exposure to the Territories; more specifically, by the essential "goodness" of the place which is best embodied in Wolf himself:

...the Territories, in spite of whatever evil they might harbor, were fundamentally good, and that he could be a part of this place anytime he wanted...that he was really no Stranger at all.... And he would have been astounded if told he had wept several times as he stood watching those great ripples chase each other toward the horizon, drinking in a sight that only a very few American children of his time had ever seen—huge empty tracts of land under a blue sky of dizzying width and breadth and, yes, even depth. It was a sky unmarked by either jet contrails across its dome or smutty bands of smog at any of its lower edges. (226-227)

The strength that maintains each of the relationships I have just described is similar to what binds Dick Hallorann to Danny Torrance in *The Shining* and Mother Abagail to the Free Zone citizens in *The Stand*. Based initially on a common danger and psychic correspondences, each of these affiliations belies a loneliness that demands love; their very existence symbolizes a disavowal of social conventions in favor of a broader-based spirit of acceptance.

Jack Torrance's psychic connection to the Overlook hotel makes him ever more self-absorbed and estranged from Wendy and Danny. Hallorann and Danny share their own spiritual bond that represents a counterbalance to the hotel's relationship with Jack. If the Overlook thrives on human malfeasance, the ability to shine encompasses the qualities of human goodness available in King's universe: loyalty and kindness, and most of all, the individual's shared responsibility for the welfare of other human beings. Late in the novel after Danny is betrayed by his natural father and besieged by the specters of the Overlook, he sends a rescue plea to Hallorann. And although the black chef briefly struggles against the summons, aware that he would be risking his life "for three white people he didn't even know," his decision is finally motivated by the power of the shining—essentially a mystical force that while somehow greater than human love, is likewise akin to it:

You could taste pain and death and tears. And now the boy was stuck in that place, and he would go. For the boy. Because, speaking to the boy, they had only been different colors when they used their mouths. So he would go. He would do what he could, because if he didn't the boy was going to die right inside his head.

But because he was human he could not help a bitter wish that the cup had never been passed his way. (316-7)

It is, moreover, the moral capacities inherent in the shining that helps Hallorann resist his own moment of temptation elicited from the hotel's dying urge to destroy Wendy and Danny (439).

The Shining is a book that illustrates the destructive presence of the past—Jack's and Wendy's relationship to their respective parents, the Overlook's unsavory history, the omnipresent reminders of Jack's alcohol abuse and his uncontrolled temper— indeed, like one of Faulkner's time-haunted novels, the past's influence in *The Shining* completely undermines whatever attempts these characters make at recreating their lives in the present. At the end of the novel, however, Hallorann has replaced Jack Torrance as Danny's surrogate father, and the black man becomes a beacon toward a new future. Breaking from Jack's obsession with history, Hallorann advises Danny to grieve for his lost father, but at the same time, to avoid repeating his father's mistake by becoming encapsulated within the events of the past. And once more King reminds us, through Hallorann's presence, that the only hope for moral survival is within a small group that sustains its identity against those forces in the world that stand in opposition to it.

"Sometimes it seems like it's only the bad people who stay healthy and prosper. The world don't love you, but your momma does and so do I. You're a good boy. You grieve for your daddy, and when you feel you have to cry over what's happened to him, you go into a closet or under your covers and cry until it's all out of you again. That's what a good son has to do. But see that you get on. That's your job in this hard world, to keep your love alive and see that you get on, no matter what. Pull your act together and just go on." (446)

Finally, Mother Abigail in *The Stand*, comprehends the full range of Flagg's evil capabilities and his ultimate intention to rule the world, but she successfully counters his secular lust through her quiet examples of endurance and love. As in *The Shining*, King suggests that love is the only way to strike some kind of balance against the active legions of evil. Unlike most of the other characters in *The Stand*, Mother Abigail has accepted the sudden demise of America, and focuses her attention on the survival of individual men and women rather than on an abstract conception of society. She is an economically disenfranchised, 108-year-old black woman whose simple belief in human worth endures long after her death, initially becoming the cultural barometer for distinguishing the Free Zone from Flagg's Las Vegas denizens. Under her visionary influence, the fledging Boulder community flourishes as an intimate utopian society; it is only after the city begins to expand with a steady influx of new citizens who have never shared direct psychic communication with Mother Abigail, that the environment begins to change for the worse.

5

King's debt to generations of literary artists in the gothic genre is obvious; this book has attempted to detail only a few of the influences and confluences that connect King to the vibrant gothic tradition. *Danse Macabre* reveals a deep reservoir of influences that stretch back to Walpole, Poe and Lovecraft, and forward to Harlan Ellison and a myriad of modern cinema directors. But certainly one of the major elements linking King's fiction to the inclusive gothic tradition is its attack on the very foundations and values upon which society is constructed. Similar to the anti-social world of the eighteenth-century gothic novel, which initiated the destruction of the cultural order and stability that characterized the Age of Reason, King's novels and stories emphasize the breakdown of civic ties, societal conventions and organizations. His work is populated with standard gothic apparatus—demons, ghosts, blood bonds with evil, self-corruption, and a reliance on supernatural terror. But in his hands these elements are frequently connected to the tragic imperfections which constrain American culture. In this sense he has, like Melville and Hawthorne a century earlier, contrived to "refine" the gothic by highlighting and advancing the sociological and philosophical implications inherent in the horror story.

Resembling Hawthorne's spirit of human forgiveness and reconciliation more than the tragic pessimism that dominates Melville's work after *Moby Dick*, King's fiction is also a reminder of what is good and noble in the human spirit. As he remarks in *Danse Macabre*, in a statement that echoes the concluding sentiments of Hawthorne in *The Scarlet Letter*, *The Marble Faun*, and "Roger Malvin's Burial,"

I believe that we are all ultimately alone and that any deep and lasting human contact is nothing more or less than a necessary illusion—but at least the feelings which we think of as "positive" and "constructive" are a reaching out, an effort to make contact and establish some sort of communication. Feelings of love and kindness, the ability to care and empathize, are all we know of the light. They are efforts to link and integrate; they are the emotions which bring us together, if not in fact then at least in a comforting illusion that makes the burden of mortality a little easier to bear. (25-6)

The moral issues presented in Stephen King's fiction connect the writer directly to Hawthorne, and by extension to the central tenets of a Judeo-Christian tradition: while we all share in the capacity for acts of evil, each of us is likewise endowed with the potential for performing good. To survive morally (and physically) individuals must cling to those human elements which thankfully distinguish us from the beasts of the night and provide a sanctuary against the various terrors which threaten to isolate the mind. King reminds us in *Danse Macabre* that morality is, after all, a "codification of those things which the heart understands to be true and those things which the heart understands to be the demands of life lived among others...civilization, in a word" (375). The moral heroes and heroines in King's world represent the most enduring aspects of human life precisely because they have learned to "live among others." This status is conferred by their resistance against selfish impulses, the will to control the urge for power, an awareness of the danger inherent in social entrapment, and most important, the ability to extend sympathy and love. Contact with worldly evil does not necessarily mean an infectuous corruption of the same magnitude; King's moral quests enlarge the spirits of his protagonists, reaffirming the Christian concept that we are finite as long as we remain isolated, but capable of greatness when we share in the capacity for love.

The moral survivors in King's canon—those young protagonists who experience not only suffering and loss, but also reconciliation and sometimes even exultation—do not allow themselves to be represented as mere victims of a malevolent or capricious power; nor is the world which they inhabit given over to darkness and despair. While King may be highly critical of the social institutions, technological toys, and warped narcissism the writer views as dominant in contemporary America, he never totally relinquishes his faith in the individual's potential for choosing good over evil. Although there may be no escape from the various horrors modern man must confront, they can still be endured. And in the course of their endurance, King's heroes and heroines attain a level of dignity commensurate with the intensity of their struggles.

Chapter 7
Conclusions and Clowns:
It as Summary
and Recapitulation

Stephen King's largest and one of his most ambitious novels to date embodies many of the core themes and issues that I have raised in preceding chapters of this book. A tale of monsters and threatened children, *It* is also a story of endurance and loyalty. And once again, as we have traced throughout King's fictional canon, the central conflict in this novel is between American adult society and the children who are neither understood nor appreciated. The five adults who survive their quest to do battle against It manage to do so because all of them are, in a manner of speaking, still children maintaining the mutual bond of love that has united them against adversity—both human and supernatural—since the time of their shared adolescence.

We have seen that the evolving patterns of evil in King's fiction most often manifest themselves in supernatural phenomena which are the consequence of human lapses in moral judgment. In tales such as "Children of the Corn," *The Shining*, and *'Salem's Lot*, maleficence is defined in terms of the "accumulated sum" of its parts: so many moments of human depravity occur in one locale over an extended period of time that evil becomes a living organism sustaining itself on historical and renewable incidents of human cruelty and violent behavior.

In the Smoke-Hole Ceremony, two members of the Losers' Club, Mike and Richie, go back to the origins of the earth in order to witness the conception of evil, the latter coinciding with the arrival of It in the center of Derry, Maine: " 'It landed right where the downtown part of Derry is now.... It's *always* been here, since the beginning of time...sleeping, maybe, waiting for the ice to melt, waiting for the people to come' " (763). Mike highlights the importance of It's relationship to the mortal world;

the creature lies dormant until humans arrive to wake it from a dark slumber. It is what the first puritan settlers might have called original sin, the principle of evil that they felt was an omnipresent component in the moral arrangement of the cosmos. As we have seen operating elsewhere in King's fiction, this principle nourishes itself on human sin, growing ever more powerful as the individual (and his community) moves further from the status of childhood and toward the corruption of adulthood.

1

Perhaps the greatest link that ties King to the late nineteenth-century naturalists—Crane, Dreiser, Norris, London—whose work so captivated King as an undergraduate, is a sense of the city as a place where human waste and confinement has reached a level in which crime and violence become its "natural" manifestations, like mold on stale bread. In his November 6, 1986 address at the University of Maine, Orono, King acknowledged that *It* specifically owed much to William Carlos Williams and Charles Dickens insofar as "the novel is an epic poem of the city as an organism." Pennywise, the clown that haunts the canals, deserted trainyards, and, most frequently, the Derry sewer system, preying on the children while inciting adults to greater levels of mayhem and violence, is the collective representation of the town's adult crimes and darkest impulses. The sewer system of any city contains the wastes of its populace; Derry's accumulative moral wastes coalesce into Pennywise.

...Derry was cold, Derry was hard, Derry didn't much give a shit if any of them lived or died, and certainly not if they triumphed over Pennywise the Clown. Derryfolk had lived with Pennywise in all his guises for a long time...and maybe, in some mad way, they had even come to understand him. To like him, need him, *Love* him? Maybe. Yes, maybe that too.... "It has been here so long that It's become a part of Derry, something as much a part of the town as the Standpipe, or the Canal, or Bassey Park, or the library. Only It's not a matter of outward geography, you understand. Maybe that was true once, but now It's...inside. Somehow It's gotten inside." (479, 503).

Every twenty-seven years Derry's " 'unusually high rate of every violent crime we know of, not excluding rape, incest, breaking and entering, auto theft, child abuse, spouse abuse, assault' " (504), reaches a point in which the clown is either strong enough (or Derry weak enough) to reactivate Pennywise.

Following a particularly gruesome outburst of communal violence, the clown resurfaces to stalk Derry's children, suggesting that this town, like the America portrayed in "Children of the Corn," must somehow compensate for its past moral transgressions by sacrificing a part of its future. Derry is indeed "a feeding place for animals" (159), possessing all the unsavory aspects of modern America found elsewhere in King's canon. Only in Derry, the vast corruption King describes in *The Talisman* or *The Stand* is narrowed to one city—concentrated and festering.

Like Faulkner's examination of Yoknapatawpha Country, King's elaborate and dark history of Derry, Maine chronicles many of the most brutal and inhumane events which have occurred during the past three centuries. And also like Faulkner, King uses specific and interrelated histories of his seven protagonists to detail the horrors that transpire daily in this closed society. Consequently, the creature that inhabits the Derry sewer system seems as much related to the environment of the town itself as Percy Grimm, Sutpen, or Flem Snopes emerge as products of Faulkner's South. The real evil in Faulkner's fiction, like King's, is social: the individual in Jefferson's society is forced to define his or her identity according to rigid distinction of race, color, geographic and family origins. These distinctions, created and nurtured by man, become the progenitors of a caste system that defines individuals principally by means of social identification. Those who can neither fit nor be fitted into the convenient categories that have been established by the people of Faulkner's towns, must be destroyed or banished from the society whose patterns of belief are threatened.

In King's fiction, the children are more often than not the outcasts, threatening the adult community—its pervasive systems of regulation and deceit. Derry's adults profess a love for their progeny, but aside from imposing an early evening curfew, there are no concrete examples of adult panic or concern surrounding the disappearance of so many young people. Indeed, the adults in this novel are most conspicuous by their absence; in the midst of Pennywise's slaughter, children remain unattended and are permitted to play in the secluded Barrens. The town has come to accept the loss of its children as a price for conducting daily business. Derry's attitude reflects its uncomfortable awareness of an insidious relationship with the clown. Bev recognizes the "thick sense of power and untinctured evil" of It in her father's moments of greatest anger: "It had been diluted somehow by her father's essential humanity—but It was here, working through him" (905). Just as the Overlook Hotel works its will through Jack Torrance, the adults of Derry are either actively engaged in performing service for Pennywise, or remain, like Mr. Ross, morally indifferent to the clown's behavior: "Beverly saw Mr. Ross getting up, looking at her, folding his paper and simply going in his house. *They won't see, they won't hear, they won't know*" (972). As Mike informs the other members of the Losers' Club upon their return to Derry, the demise of so many town children has not appeared on national news because neither the city nor the creature that feeds upon it wants the information revealed (503).

Hawthorne and his puritan ancestors would have understood most thoroughly Pennywise's relationship with the town of Derry. They knew evil as an element that pervades everything human—from the community itself to the individuals who guide it. Anytime any act of violence or cruelty occurs in Derry, Pennywise is present to celebrate it, to participate in it, and to reap the power accrued from the act itself. When the Bradley gang is slaughtered in the center of town by the citizens of Derry, the clown is a member of the righteous mob, emptying her own bullets from a smoking rifle (653). Similarly, when the Black Spot is torched by a legion of racial bigots, Pennywise is there in the guise of a giant bird of prey, " 'big bunches of balloons tied to each wing, and it floated' " (470).

The spontaneous explosion of the Kitchener Ironworks that results in the deaths of many unsuspecting children who are searching for Easter eggs within its bowels is tied to Derry and the clown that punishes the city at the same time as it represents it. Both the ironworks disaster and Pennywise herself prey upon the vulnerability of children. Under the veneer of Pennywise's games and promises lurks the reality of deception and slaughter. The adult citizens of Derry mirror this very tendency in their daily behavior toward their children. Bev's father, for example, abuses his daughter in physical beatings that barely mask his repressed incestuous urges. He has done permanent psychological damage to her, as her eventual choice of marriage to Tom is simply a continuation of the violent pattern that originated with her father and extends beyond him to Pennywise the Dancing Clown. While she is the most explicit illustration of Derry's destructive attitude toward its children, the other young people in the novel have suffered similar fates: Henry Bowers owes his psychopathic behavior to his father's many drunken examples;

to keep Eddie Kaspbrak forever dependent upon her, his mother convinces him that he is a frail boy who dares not leave home without his aspirator; Ben Hanscom's self-image remains negative because of his mother's need to judge his affection for her by the amount of food he ingests; and Bill Denbrough tries in vain to recapture his parents' interest after the death of his younger brother. In the course of the novel, Eddie Kaspbrak and his fellow members of the Losers' Club "discover one of childhood's great truths. *Grownups are the real monsters*" (772). Like the adults in King's novella *The Body*, Derry's grownups don't really "see" their own children, or if they do, it is only long enough to abuse them; ironically, Derry's children are the only ones capable of seeing Pennywise and the gory remains of her victims.

King's choice of a clown as a unifying symbol for the various creatures representing It is masterful: what better lure for a child than the carnival clown—an adult in elaborate make-up—who is capable of disguising monstrous intentions. When Stan encounters Pennywise for the first time as a child, he is attracted to the creature by the sound of calliope music. As the boy draws nearer to the steel Standpipe, "the calliope music had gotten suddenly louder, as if to mask the sound of footsteps." The work "mask" is important here as it appropriately signifies the role of the clown throughout the novel: her viciousness is "masked" under the promise of false joy. Pennywise attracts all children to her by preying upon the youthful recollections of summer carnivals, "conjuring up trace memories which were as delightful as they were ephemeral" (423). In actuality, however, the clown, mirroring the spirit of the town she embodies, scorns innocence; her real purpose, like the "Heaven" described in Emily Dickinson's own poem on carnivals "I've known a Heaven, like a Tent," is to deliver only death and negation:

The calliope music had gotten louder yet. It drifted and echoed down the spiral staircase. There was nothing cheery about it now. It had changed. It had become a dirge. It screamed like wind and water, and in the mind's eye Stan saw a county fair at the end of autumn, wind and rain blowing up a deserted midway, pennons flapping, tents bulging, falling over, wheeling away like canvas bats. He saw empty rides standing against the sky like scaffolds; the wind drummed and hooted in the weird angles of their struts. He suddenly understood that death was in this place with him, that death was coming for him out of the dark and he could not run. (424-425)

2

It is not one of Stephen King's finest novels; the book possesses neither the thematic and philosophical depth of *The Stand,* the concise focus of *Pet Sematary,* nor the sustained terror of *The Shining.* But *It* does represent one of King's most ambitious stylistic endeavors. As early as *Carrie,* King evinced an interest in experimenting with narrative forms. *The Stand*'s multiple story lines, which produce an initial sense of confusion in the reader, eventually coalesce into a single theme: the allegorical battle between good and evil. In many of his fictional works, King freely uses experimental stylistic devices—the stream of consciousness, interior monologues, multiple narrators, and a juggling of time sequences—in order to draw the reader into a direct and thorough involvement with the characters and events of the tale.

In a 1986 interview with Burton Hatlen, King's former professor informed me that as an undergraduate King was intrigued with the novels of William Faulkner and that "he spent one year reading everything he [Faulkner] ever wrote." I have already mentioned a possible Faulknerian influence in *It*'s portrait of a regional evil and the generational corruption that is associated with It, but an awareness of the Southern writer is also apparent in King's stylistic efforts. In *The Sound and the Fury,* perhaps Faulkner's best work in terms of stylistic innovations, the writer eclipses a traditional succession of events by the careful interplay of leitmotifs that serve to disrupt the logical passage from one moment to another. He chooses to dispense with the typical characteristics that are found in conventional narratives—a linear plot development and chronological character growth—in order to show the internal workings of the mind. The demise of the Compson family is told backwards through a series of recollections, reflections, and remembrances, instead of through a logical pattern of rising actions.

King employs a similar interrupted narrative style throughout *It,* as the history of the Losers' Club and the monster that is the town of Derry is slowly and thoroughly made clear for the reader in a series of dramatic childhood flashbacks and recapitulations. The actions of the present are held in suspension for the length of long clarifying flashbacks in a way that vividly recalls Faulkner's techniques of stylistic experimentation. The inversion of the years 1958 and 1985 reflects King's structural efforts throughout the novel to juxtapose past with present. As the quest to destroy It intensifies, forcing the six adults to recall their adolescent encounters with the monster, the specific time frames of 1958 and 1985 blur, becoming nearly inseparable. Indeed, the last quarter of the book mirrors this focus as the varying time references of individual chapters literally flow into one another making memory and reality synonymous.

In attempting to penetrate the myth of a complicated Southern past, Quentin Compson and his friend Shreve in *Absalom, Absalom!* must synthesize the diverse and subjective interpretations of Miss Rosa, Quentin's father, and his grandfather. Quentin is forced into such an intimate involvement with the flow of words and concepts that he, like the reader, becomes almost unaware of time sequence or the chronological relativity of events. In King's novel, a similar process is at work as the individual members of the Losers' Club struggle to piece together a collective twenty-seven year memory that none of them understands completely. King highlights their quest in a series of clarifying flashbacks that bridges the gap of history. Aside from establishing the timelessness of It as well as the timelessness of childhood fears, King's experimentation with spatial relationships is also meant to underscore the only hope these child-adults possess in their struggle against Pennywise: that their link to one another and a collective adolescent imagination can be re-established quickly enough to destroy the creature:

None of those things have to be said, perhaps, and the reason why they don't has already been stated: they still love one another. Things have changed over the last twenty-seven years, but that, miraculously, hasn't. It is, Mike thinks, our only real hope.

The only thing that really remains is to finish going through it, to complete the job of catching up, of stapling the past to present so that the strip of experience forms some half-assed kind of wheel. Yes, Mike thinks, that's it. Tonight the job is to make the wheel; tomorrow we can see if it still turns.... (702)

As Thomas R. Edwards remarked in his review of the novel in a recent issue of *The New York Review of Books,* "Only brave and imaginative children, or adults who learn to remember and honor their childish selves, can hope to foil It" (58).

3

Ben Hanscom's favorite recollection of his childhood in Derry is the public library. Not only do his memories of pleasant days within its doors contrast with his larger perspective of life in the town, but the physical structure of the place itself—especially the glassed-in corridor that connects the child and adult sections of the library—has exerted a profound influence over Hanscom's architectural career. The glass corridor served as an inspiration for his first major office building, constructed in London. But even more relevant to the return of Ben and his friends to Derry is the use of the corridor image as a metaphor for the novel's quest to recapture the past.

> He walked across the library lawn, barely noticing that his dress boots were getting wet, to have a look at that glassed-in pasageway between the grownups' library and the Children's Library. It was also unchanged, and from here, standing just outside the bowed branches of a weeping willow tree, he could see people passing back and forth.... The magic was that glowing cylinder of light and life connecting those two dark buildings like a lifeline, the magic was in watching people walk through it across the dark snowfield, untouched by either the dark or the cold. It made them lovely and Godlike.... The force of memory almost dizzied him for a moment as he stepped into the mild light of the hanging glass globes. The force was not physical—not like a shot to the jaw or a slap. It was more akin to that queer feeling of time doubling back on itself that people call, for want of a better term, *deja-vu*. Ben had had the feeling before, but it had never struck him with such disorienting power; for the moment or two he stood inside the door, he felt literally lost in time, not really sure how old he was. Was he thirty-eight or eleven? (536-538)

Analogous to the manner in which this fragile glass conduit bridges the gap between the adult and child sections of the library, in the course of this novel the members of the Losers' Club move between the two worlds of their remembered childhood and present adulthood to re-establish their own "magic lifeline." Just as the observed rainbow in William Wordsworth's "My Heart Leaps Up" serves as a connecting point between "when my life began/ So it is now I am a man," Hascom's passageway represents the possibility for adult self-renovation that is available in the recollection of adolescent memories. As we discussed in Chapter 6 while considering other examples of corridor metaphors in King's fiction, the passageway from innocence to experience is a crucial one for many of his characters; those who pass through this symbolic corridor to sever completely their connection to childhood are doomed to the isolated sterility of adulthood. The ideal condition, as King symbolizes in the above excerpt, seems to be within the individual's ability for keeping open the passageway that connects adolescence to adulthood. This is, of course, why Ben and his long-lost friends must return to Derry:

to defeat It once and for all the Losers' Club must reopen their personal and collective conduits to childhood.

Although each of the Losers is highly successful financially (except for Mike, who has chosen to remain in Derry), their childless marriages have allowed them to maintain a connection to " 'some sort of group will' " (516) associated with their shared adolescence. Their recollected loyalty, coupled with a willingness to sacrifice individual volitions and, as it turns out, lives for the welfare of each other, insulates these five men and one woman from the traits of selfishness and immorality that are usually synonymous with King's descriptions of adulthood.

The adult-children of this novel do battle against It not only for purposes of self-preservation. Bill wishes to avenge his brother's death, but he and the others also seem genuinely disposed toward saving the lives of Derry's children. Like Gordie and Chris in *The Body*, they establish a level of identification with other adolescents as a result of their own vulnerability. The Losers likewise resemble Jack Sawyer in *The Talisman*, insofar as they are united in a quest to vanquish evil for reasons that are nobler than themselves. Moreover, their purpose for doing so is related to a set of clearly delineated moral principles that are perhaps best understood by children: Pennywise has been bad and she must be punished.

Just as Pennywise gains a kind of supernatural energy from the sins of Derry's adults, the potency of their collective love allows the Losers to perform courageous acts against forces more powerful than their individual selves. As we discussed in examining Danny Torrance's relationship with Hallorann in *The Shining* and Jack Sawyer's bond with Speedy and Wolf in *The Talisman*, there is a power in love that is stronger than the malevolent energies King associates with evil. In *It*, Mike Hanlon's father imparts to his son the same sense of continuity, courage and hope that the latter will employ in order to re-establish the bond of love among the Losers. Mike's father is certainly an illustration of how an adult might maintain a loving and positive link to his children as well as to his own childhood. In this sense, Mike's relationship with his father—and by extension, his father's recollections of Dick Hallorann's bravery the night The Black Spot burned (465-6)—become the models upon which the Losers will base their own selfless commitment to one another. The act of sexual intercourse that Beverly shares with each member of the Losers' Club after their initial battle against It in the summer of 1958 cements their union; she becomes the center of their magic circle, and serves as an effective feminine force to counterbalance the evil of the female It. Although Beverly is childless, her friends become her surrogate children; she protects and comforts each of them throughout the book. When Eddie Kaspbrak dies at the end of the novel, it is in her arms, and she offers him a final repose in imagery reminiscent of the Pietà. In contrast to Beverly, It is pregnant, but her children are doomed. As It flees from Bill and Richie, eggs are discarded haphazardly, left to be crushed under the bootheels of Ben Hanscom. Evil dies as it chooses to live: without regard for anyone or anything beyond itself.

As a child, Bill Denbrough was capable of defeating It in the Ritual of Chüd. He accomplished this essentially by himself; his motivation for avenging his brother's death combined with the enormous powers of his eleven year-old imagination, allowed him to vanquish the transmogrified Spider-It even in its own lair. But as an adult, twenty-seven years later, his powers have diminished considerably. As Beverly postulates earlier in explaining Stan's suicide, " 'Maybe that's why he killed himself. Maybe he understood that if there was magic, it wouldn't work for grownups' " (516). Consequently, to destroy It a final time, Bill requires the direct intercession of Richie and Eddie. Without their assistance, It would have killed him:

It wanted...to break their mental communication. If that ceased, he would be utterly destroyed. To pass beyond communication was to pass beyond salvation; he understood that much from the way his parents had behaved toward him after George had died. (1055)

On two separate occasions a young boy fearlessly rides his skateboard in front of Bill while pointing out that " 'you can't be careful on a skateboard' " (1109). Bill and his friends come to employ the same spirit of adolescent abandonment in their assault against It. They are inspired by a child's righteous indignation toward the monster's callous actions. As a result of their spontaneous concern for each other, they overcome the adult fear that results in Stan's suicide and produces their own initial apprehensiveness upon returning to Derry. His renewed contact with the recuperative powers of childhood also enables Denbrough to rescue his wife from a catatonic state after her encounter with It. Dressed in clothes that are reminiscent of his youth, Bill rides with Audra on his bicycle "to beat the devil" one last time. Just as his adolescent friends have helped him to retrieve his past to defeat It, Bill's renewed commitment to "the mystery of childhood" (1138) allows him to partake of the mystical energy Ben Hanscom first perceived in the glass-doomed corridor of the library.

King's belief in the spiritual importance of adults maintaining a child-like faith in the magic of life is directly relevant to the many references to rock music which appear in *It*. Throughout King's fiction it is possible to trace a strong association among adolescence, automobiles, and rock music. In *Christine*, for example, each chapter heading makes use of rock lyrics from songs written about cars. Until *It*, however, King's frequent references to this music usually appear to highlight or foreshadow sinister events; as Christine becomes more diabolical, the lyrical allusions reflect the novel's impending doom, becoming darker, more ominous. In *It*, on the other hand, King employs rock and roll as yet another means to illustrate the dynamism of youth. A fundamental premise of rock music is its commitment to sustaining the magic of adolescence, even into adulthood. This concern has been a guiding force in rock since its inception, and it is especially prevalent in songs by The Who, The Doors, and Bruce Springsteen, all of whom are some of King's favorite artists. But Bob Seger perhaps best defines the recuperative powers of rock music in lyrics that suggest its perpetual affiliation with youthful exuberance:

You're a little bit older
And a lot less bolder than you use to be,
Sweet sixteen's turned thirty-one
You need a little fix when the workday's done...
Come back, baby
Rock-n-roll never forgets.

Richie "Records" Tozier's role in *It* is interesting in light of this discussion, as his contact with rock music extends from his association with the Losers to his current adult occupation as an L.A. disc jockey. His connection to music has allowed him to maintain a fresh and dynamic perspective on life. Indeed, he possesses the same bravado and self-assertiveness that are characteristic of the rock era; and these elements are not only instrumental to the final destruction of It, they also help Richie to survive. In contrast to the adults of Derry, who, like Richie's and Bill Denbrough's mothers, are "death on rock and roll," Richie obtains a strength from the music that ties him not only to the world's losers, but also to the world's children: "There was a power in that music, a power which seemed to most rightfully belong to all the skinny kids, fat kids, ugly kids, shy kids—the world's losers, in short" (582). For Richie, as well as for King, rock music is more than a good beat; it is a means of communicating a sense of personal and collective disenfranchisement, of identifying with a source of power, and of transcending the self's limitations on a current of rhythm and energy: "In it he felt a mad hilarious voltage which had the power to both kill and exalt" (582). In essence, Richie's response to rock and roll parallels Ben Hascom's magic corridor. It is therefore no mere coincidence that Bill Denbrough's transformation at the novel's conclusion, which allows him to rescue Audra at the same time as he rescues his nexus to youth, is subtly aligned with the mysterious energies of rock and roll:

> She pushed him away so she could look at him. "Bill, are you still stuttering?"
> "No," Bill said, and kissed her. "My stutter is gone."
> "For good?"
> "Yes," he said. "I think this time it's gone for good."
> "Did you say something about rock and roll?"
> "I don't know. Did I?"
> "I love you," she said.
> He nodded and smiled. When he smiled he looked very young, bald head or not. "I love you too," he said. And what else counts?" (1137-1138)

4

In "Tintern Abbey," "Ode: Intimations of Immortality," and *The Prelude*, William Wordsworth advises the adult to retain an active memory of his childhood in order to cope with the "evil tongues, / Rash judgments, the sneers of selfish men...where no kindness is" ("Tintern Abbey," 11. 128-130). Though no longer a child, it is possible for the adult to watch and hear with sympathetic eyes and ears. Moreover, the adult may not share the uncomplicated joys of childhood, but he can find moral strength in retaining the values learned as an adolescent.

The neo-Wordsworthian vision of hope that animates the entire girth of *It* reaffirms the pattern for survival we have traced in King's novels and tales. In one of his diary entries, Mike Hanlon argues that "It protects Itself by the simple fact that as the children grow into adults, they become either incapable of faith or crippled by a sort of spiritual and imaginative arthritis" (894). This position is certainly in evidence throughout King's work, but so is its antithesis: that adult perspectives do not have to narrow; that faith in the magic of life, which makes both life and magic possible, does not have to disappear with the loss of childhood. It seems equally clear, however, that to sustain the metaphor of Ben Hanscom's "glowing cylinder of light and life," adults need to maintain their connection to adolescence—especially the capacity to accept and give love. As Wordsworth tells us in the First Book of *The Prelude*, "my hope has been, that I might fetch/ Invigorating thoughts from former years" (11. 62-622).

King's romantic perception of childhood offers to light the way to moral excellence by helping man to distinguish between, and understand the nature of, good and evil. As Bill Denbrough comes fully to understand at the conclusion of *It*, the imaginative faith of childhood was given to man to guide him through life. It can help him envision the moral constitution of the world; it can explain the nature of the human animal and its natural imperfections; it can even lead him to the threshold of recreating his personality and identity.

Stephen King grew up without a father, and the absence of this relationship in his real life may have given impetus to the fictional creation of his "alternative families." However, if these non-traditional families—the Losers' Club, and the pairings of Jack and Speedy, Danny and Hallorann—were simply autobiographical statements of the writer's broken childhood, the recollection of what these characters mutually experienced would not continue to endure for the reader. Abandoned by governmental bureaucracies and the nuclear family itself, King's small non-traditional alliances represent the light in the darkness of his social landscape. His heroes and heroines establish character unions that embody the spiritual essence of Ben Hascom's symbolic corridor, as the relationships which endure in King's world most often appear to consist of a melding of child with adult. The resulting synthesis produces individuals who possess the courage to vanquish worldly evil because of their sustained association with the magical powers of youth. While traditional families and societal relationships may not endure in King's landscape of fear, his protagonists are endowed with alternatives to these fractured institutions that represent not only the hope for survival, but also the dream of salvation.

References Cited

Allen, Dick, ed.. *Science-Fiction: The Future*. New York: Harcourt, Brace, Jovanovich, 1983.

Bosky, Bernadette. "Stephen King and Peter Straub: Fear and Friendship" in *Discovering Stephen King*, ed. Darrell Schweitzer. Mercer Island, WA: Starmont House, 1985.

_____ "The Mind's a Monkey: Character and Psychology in Stephen King's Recent Fiction" in *Kingdom of Fear: The World of Stephen King*, eds. Tim Underwood and Chuck Miller. New York: New American Library, 1986.

Bradley, A.C.. *Shakespearean Tragedy*. Greenwich, CT: Fawcett, 1904.

Brown, Stephen P.. "The Life and Death of Richard Bachman: Stephen King's Doppelganger" in *Kingdom of Fear: The World of Stephen King*, eds. Tim Underwood and Chuck Miller. New York: New American Library, 1986.

Chase, Richard. *The American Novel and its Tradition*. New York: Doubleday, 1957.

Collings, Michael and David Engebretson. *The Shorter Works of Stephen King*. Mercer Island, WA: Starmont House, 1985.

De Tocqueville, Alexis. *Democracy in America*. New York: Doubleday, 1969.

Edwards, Thomas, R.. Review of *It*, by Stephen King. *New York Review of Books*, 18 December 1986, 58-59.

Eliot, T.S.. *The Waste Land and Other Poems*. New York: Harcourt, Brace, 1934.

Ellison, Harlan. "Harlan Ellison's Watching" in *Kingdom of Fear: The World of Stephen King*, eds. Tim Underwood and Chuck Miller. New York: New American Library, 1986.

Fiedler, Leslie. *Love and Death in the American Novel*. New York: Stein and Day, 1966.

Frank, Frederick, S.. "The Gothic Romance" in *Horror Literature: A Historical Survey and Critical Guide to the Best of Horror*, ed. Marshall B. Tymn. New York: The Bowker Company, 1981.

Frazer, James. *The Golden Bough*. New York: Macmillan, 1951.

Habermas, Jurgen. *Theory and Practice*. Trans. John Viertel. Boston: Beacon Press, 1973.

Hatlen, Burton. "Beyond the Kittery Bridge: Stephen King's Maine" in *Fear Itself*, eds. Tim Underwood and Chuck Miller. New York: New American Library, 1985.

Hawthorne, Nathaniel. *The Marble Faun* in *The Complete Novels and Selected Tales of Nathaniel Hawthorne*. New York: Random House, 1937.

Herron, Don. "The Biggest Horror Fan of Them All" in *Discovering Stephen King*, ed. Darrell Schweitzer. Mercer Island, WA: Starmont House, 1985.

Indick, Ben. "King and the Literary Tradition of Horror and the Supernatural" in *Fear Itself*, eds. Tim Underwood and Chuck Miller. New York: New American Library, 1985.

Jackson, Shirley. *The Haunting of Hill House*. New York: Viking, 1959.

King, Stephen. *Apt Pupil* in *Different Seasons*. New York: Viking, 1982.

————. "Battleground" in *Night Shift*. New York: New American Library, 1979.

———. "Before the Play." *Whispers* 17/18 (August 1982): 19-47.

————. *Carrie*. New York: New American Library, 1974.

————. "Children of the Corn" in *Night Shift*. New York: New American Library, 1979.

————. *Christine*. New York: Viking, 1983.

————. *Cycle of the Werewolf*. Westland, MI: Land of Enchantment, 1983.

————. *Danse Macabre*. New York: Viking, 1983.

————. *Firestarter*. New York: Viking, 1980.

————. *It*. New York: Viking, 1986.

————. "On The Shining and Other Perpetrations." *Whispers* 17/18 (August 1982): 11-16.

————. *Pet Sematary*. New York: Doubleday, 1983.

————. *The Body* in *Different Seasons*. New York: Viking, 1982.

————. "The Boogeyman" in *Night Shift*. New American Library, 1979.

————. "The Last Rung on the Ladder" in *Night Shift*. New York: New American Library, 1979.

————. "The Ledge" in *Night Shift*. New York: New American Library, 1979.

————. "The Mist" in *Skeleton Crew*. New York: Putnam's, 1985.

————. "The Monkey" in *Skeleton Crew*. New York: Putnam's 1985.

————. "The Raft" in *Skeleton Crew*. New York: Putnam's, 1985.

————. *The Shining*. New York: New American Library, 1978.

————. *The Stand*. New York: New American Library, 1979.

————. *The Talisman*. New York: Berkley, 1985.

————. "Trucks" in *Night Shift*. New York: New American Library, 1979.

————. "Strawberry Spring" in *Night Shift*. New York: New American Library, 1979.

————. "Uncle Otto's Truck" in *Skeleton Crew*. New York: Putnam's, 1985.

Klavan, Andrew. "The Pleasure of the Subtext: Stephen King's Id-Life Crisis." *Village Voice*, 3 March 1987, 46.

Lasch, Christopher. *The Culture of Narcissism*. New York: Norton, 1979.

Mailer, Norman. *Of a Fire on the Moon*. Boston: Little, Brown, 1970.

Manchel, Frank. *An Album of Modern Horror Films*. New York: Franklin Watts, 1983.

Melville, Herman. *Moby-Dick; or, the White Whale*. New York: Penguin, 1972.

Nelson, Thomas Allen. *Kubrick: Inside the Artist's Maze.* Bloomington, Indiana: University of Indiana Press, 1982.

Shelley, Mary. *Frankenstein.* London: Oxford University Press, 1969.

Wager, Walter. Review of *It*, by Stephen King. *The New York Times Book Review*, 24 August 1986, 9.

Weston, Jessie. *From Ritual to Romance.* New York: Macmillan, 1951.

Winter, Douglas, ed.. *Faces of Fear.* New York: Berkley Books, 1985.

_____ *Stephen King: The Art of Darkness.* New York: New American Library, 1984.

_____ "The Funhouse of Fear." *Fantasy Review* 95 (October 1986): 15-16.

Wood, Robin. "Cat and Dog: Lewis Teague's Stephen King Novels." *Action* 2 (Fall 1985): 39-45.

Wordsworth, William. *Poetical Works*, eds. E. de Selincourt and Helen Darbishire. New York: Oxford University Press, 1940-1945.

Stephen King:
A Guide to Scholarship,
1980-1987

Compiled by Marshall B. Tymn

This bibliography is a comprehensive survey of academic scholarship on Stephen King, and does not generally cite articles in newspapers, popular magazines, or fan publications; nor does it cite reviews and interviews. All book-length studies are annotated. For a detailed listing of the items I have omitted, see Michael R. Collings' excellent *The Annotated Guide to Stephen King* (Starmont House, 1986).

Alexander, Alex E. "Stephen King's *Carrie*: A Universal Fairytale." *Journal of Popular Culture*, 13 (1980).

Barker, Clive. "Surviving the Ride." In *Kingdom of Fear* (see main entry, Underwood/Miller).

Bloch, Robert. "Monsters in Our Midst." In *Kingdom of Fear* (see main entry, Underwood/Miller).

Bosky, Bernadette Lynn. "The Mind's a Monkey: Character and Psychology in Stephen King's Recent Fiction." In *Kingdom of Fear* (see main entry, Underwood/Miller).

———. "Stephen King and Peter Straub: Fear and Friendship." In *Discovering Stephen King* (see main entry, Schweitzer).

Brown, Stephen P. "The Life and Death of Richard Bachman: Stephen King's Doppelganger." In *Kingdom of Fear* (see main entry, Underwood/Miller).

Browne, Ray and Gary Hoppenstand, eds. *The Gothic World of Stephen King: Landscape of Nightmares*. Bowling Green, OH: Bowling Green State Univ. Popular Press, 1987. (Not seen.)

Campbell, Ramsey. "Welcome to Room 217." In *Kingdom of Fear* (see main entry, Underwood/Miller).

Cheever, Leonard. "Apocalypse and the Popular Imagination: Stephen King's *The Stand*." *RE: Artes Liberales*, 8 (Fall 1981).

Collings, Michael R. *The Annotated Guide to Stephen King: A Primary and Secondary Bibliography of the Works of America's Premier Horror Writer*. Starmont Reference Guide, No. 8. Mercer Island, WA: Starmont House, 1986. Annotations cover King's own works, major articles about King, and review.

———. *The Films of Stephen King*. Starmont Studies in Literary Criticism, No. 12. Mercer Island, WA: Starmont House, 1986. A history and analysis of King's role as a filmmaker.

_____ *The Many Facets of Stephen King.* Starmont Studies in Literary Criticism, No. 11. Mercer Island, WA: Starmont House, 1985. A look at King the artist, the critic, and the social phenomenon.

_____ *"The Stand:* Science Fiction into Fantasy." In *Discovering Stephen King* (see main entry, Schweitzer).

_____ *Stephen King as Richard Bachman.* Starmont Studies in Literary Criticism, No. 10. Mercer Island, WA: Starmont House, 1985. Critical evaluation of five works published under the Bachman pseudonym.

_____ *The Stephen King Phenomenon.* Starmont Studies in Literary Criticism, No. 14. Mercer Island, WA: Starmont House, 1987. Examines King from multiple perspectives, including the themes, images, patterns, and characters he has explored since *Carrie.* Comments on King's influence on contemporary publishing.

_____ and David Engelbretson. *The Shorter Works of Stephen King.* Starmont Studies in Literary Criticism, No. 9. Mercer Island, WA: Starmont House, 1985. A comprehensive study of King's shorter fiction, from single stories to full collections.

Conner, Jeff. *Stephen King Goes to Hollywood: A Lavishly Illustrated Guide to All the Films Based on Stephen King's Fiction.* New York: New American Library, 1987.

Crawford, Gary William. "Stephen King's American Gothic." In *Discovering Stephen King* (see main entry, Schweitzer).

D'Ammassa, Don. "Three by Bachman." In *Discovering Stephen King* (see main entry, Schweitzer).

Egan, James. "Antidetection: Gothic and Detective Conventions in the Fiction of Stephen King." *Clue: A Journal of Detection,* 4 (1984).

_____ "Apocalypticism in the Fiction of Stephen King." *Extrapolation,* 25 (1984).

_____ " 'A Single Powerful Spectacle': Stephen King's Gothic Melodrama." *Extrapolation,* 27 (1986).

Ehlers, Leigh A. *"Carrie:* Book and Film." *Literature Film Quarterly* (Spring 1981). Rpt. *Ideas of Order in Literature and Film.* Ed. Peter Ruppert. Talahassie, FL: University of Florida Press, 1980.

Ellison, Harlan. "Two Selections from Harlan Ellison's Watching." In *Kingdom of Fear* (see main entry, Underwood/Miller).

Fiedler, Leslie. "Fantasy as Commodity and Myth." In *Kingdom of Fear* (see main entry, Underwood/Miller).

Gibbs, Kenneth. "Stephen King and the Traditions of American Gothic." *Gothic,* 1 (1986).

Grant, Charles L. "The Gray Arena." In *Fear Itself* (see main entry, Underwood/Miller).

Greeley, Andrew M. "Stephen King's Horror Has a Healing Power." In *Kingdom of Fear* (see main entry, Underwood/Miller).

Heldreth, Leonard G. "The Ultimate Horror: The Dead Child in Stephen King's Stories and Novels." In *Discovering Stephen King* (see main entry, Schweitzer).

Herron, Don. "The Biggest Horror Fan of Them All." In *Discovering Stephen King* (see main entry, Schweitzer).

_____ "King: The Good, the Bad and the Academic." In *Kingdom of Fear* (see main entry, Underwood/Miller).

——— "Horror Springs in the Fiction of Stephen King." In *Fear Itself* (see main entry, Underwood/Miller).

Horstling, Jessie. *Stephen King at the Movies.* New York: Signet/Starlog, 1986. Includes King's responses to films made from his works, plus several interviews; contains 60 pages of color stills.

Indick, Ben P. "King and the Literary Tradition of Horror and the Supernatural." In *Fear Itself* (see main entry, Underwood/Miller).

——— "King as a Writer for Children." In *Kingdom of Fear* (see main entry, Underwood/Miller).

——— "Stephen King As an Epic Writer." In *Discovering Stephen King* (see main entry, Schweitzer).

Ketchum, Marty, Daniel J.H. Levack, and Jeff Levin. "Stephen King: A Bibliography." In *Fear Itself* (see main entry, Underwood/Miller).

King, Stephen. *Bare Bones: Talking Terror with Stephen King.* San Francisco: Underwood-Miller, 1987 (Not seen).

——— "The Horror Writer and the Ten Bears." In *Kingdom of Fear* (see main entry, Underwood/Miller).

Larson, Randall D. "*Cycle of the Werewolf* and the Moral Tradition of Horror." In *Discovering Stephen King* (see main entry, Schweitzer).

Leiber, Fritz. "Horror Hits a High." In *Fear Itself* (see main entry, Underwood/Miller).

Lidston, Robert. "*Dracula* and *'Salem's Lot*: Why the Monsters Won't Die." *West Virginia University Philological Papers*, 28 (1982).

McDowell, Michael. "The Unexpected and the Inevitable." In *Kingdom of Fear* (see main entry, Underwood/Miller).

McGuire, Karen. "The Artist as Demon in Mary Shelley, Stevenson, Walpole, Stoker, and King." *Gothic*, 1 (1986).

Magistrale, Tony. "Crumbling Castles of Sand: The Social Landscapes of Stephen King's Gothic Vision," *Journal of Popular Literature*, 1 (1985).

——— "Inherited Haunts: Stephen King's Terrible Children." *Extrapolation*, 26 (1985).

Mechkow, Sanford Z. "Synopses of Stephen King's Fiction." In *Discovering Stephen King* (see main entry, Schweitzer).

Meyer, Richard E. "Stephen King." In *Beacham's Popular Fiction in America*, Vol. 2. Ed. Walter Beacham. Washington: Beacham Publishing Company, 1985.

Miller, Chuck. "Stephen King Goes to the Movies." In *Kingdom of Fear* (see main entry, Underwood/Miller).

Minifie, Don. "A Gift to Frighten: The Films of Stephen King." *Films & Filming*, No. 369 (1985).

Monteleone, Thomas F. "King's Characters: The Main(e) Heat." In *Kingdom of Fear* (see main entry, Underwood/Miller).

Neilson, Keith. "*The Dead Zone*." In *Magill's Literary Annual 1980*, Vol. 1. Ed. Frank N. Magill, Englewood Cliffs, NJ: Salem Press, 1980.

Nolan, William F. "The Good Fabric: Of Night Shifts and Skeleton Crews." In *Kingdom of Fear* (see main entry, Underwood/Miller).

Notkin, Deborah L. "Stephen King: Horror and Humanity for Our Time." In *Fear Itself* (see main entry, Underwood/Miller).

Patrouch, Joseph F. Jr. "Stephen King in Context." In *Patterns of the Fantastic: Academic Programming at Chicon IV*. Ed. Donald M. Hassler, Mercer Island, WA: Starmont House, 1983.

Platt, Charles. "Stephen King." *Dream Makers II*. New York: Berkeley, 1983; rev. ed. New York: Ungar, 1987.

Price, Robert M. "Stephen King and the Lovecraft Mythos." In *Discovering Stephen King* (see main entry, Schweitzer).

Ryan, Alan. "The Marsten House in *'Salem's Lot*." In *Fear Itself* (see main entry, Underwood/Miller).

Schneider, Peter. "Collecting the Works of Stephen King." *AB Bookman's Weekly*, 72 (1983).

Schweitzer, Darrell. "Collecting Stephen King." In *Discovering Stephen King* (see main entry, Schweitzer).

_____, ed. *Discovering Stephen King*. Starmont Studies in Literary Criticism, No. 8. Mercer Island, WA: Starmont House, 1985. Original essays by academics on King's work.

Scott, Pete. "Stephen King: The Shadow Exploded." *Dark Horizons*, No. 25 (1982).

Streiber, Whitley. "Thanks to the Crypt-Keeper." In *Kingdom of Fear* (see main entry, Underwood/Miller).

Stump, Debra. "A Matter of Choice: King's *Cujo* and Malamud's *The Natural*." In *Discovering Stephen King* (see main entry, Schweitzer).

_____ "Stephen King with a Twist: The E.C. Influence." In *Discovering Stephen King* (see main entry, Schweitzer).

Thompson, Bill. "A Girl Named Carrie." In *Kingdom of Fear* (see main entry, Underwood/Miller).

Tymn, Marshall B. "Stephen King: A Bibliography." In *Discovering Stephen King* (see main entry, Schweitzer).

Underwood, Tim. "The Skull Beneath the Skin." In *Kingdom of Fear* (see main entry, Underwood/Miller).

_____ and Chuck Miller, eds. *Fear Itself: The Horror Fiction of Stephen King*. San Francisco: Underwood-Miller, 1982; rpt. New York: New American Library/Signet, 1985. The first book to examine the entire scope of King's literature, from his short stories published before his first novel, *Carrie*, through his popular novels, to his most recent books, *Cujo* and *The Dark Tower*. This anthology collects nine original and reprinted essays and contains a bibliographical checklist of King's stories, books, and articles.

_____ eds. *Kingdom of Fear: The World of Stephen King*. San Francisco: Underwood-Miller, 1986; rpt. New York: New American Library/Signet, 1987. Seventeen original essays and introductions about King, his novels and stories.

Warren, Alan. "Has Success Spoiled Steven King?" In *Discovering Stephen King* (see main entry, Schweitzer).

Warren, Bill. "The Movies and Mr. King." In *Fear Itself* (see main entry, Underwood/Miller).

Williamson, Chet. "The Early Tales: Stephen King and *Startling Mystery Stories*." In *Discovering Stephen King* (see main entry, Schweitzer).

Winter, Douglas E. "The Night Journeys of Stephen King." In *Fear Itself* (see main entry, Underwood/Miller).

_____ *Faces of Fear: Encounters with the Creators of Modern Horror.* New York: Berkley, 1985. Interviews with 17 well-known writers of horror fiction, including King.

_____ *Stephen King.* Starmont Reader's Guide, No. 16. Mercer Island, WA: Starmont House, 1982. A chronology of King's life and works, chapters on the novels and stories, plus primary and secondary bibliographies.

_____ *Stephen King: The Art of Darkness.* New York: New American Library, 1984; expanded and updated, 1986.

_____ "Stephen King, Peter Straub and the Quest of *The Talisman.*" *Twilight Zone Magazine* (February 1985).

_____ "Stephen King's Art of Darkness: The First Decade." *Fantasy Review,* No. 73 (1984).

Wolfe, Gary K. "Strange Invaders: An Essay-Review." *Modern Fiction Studies* (Spring 1986).

Yarbro, Chelsea Quinn. "Cinderella's Revenge—Twists on Fairy Tale and Mythic Themes in the Work of Stephen King." In *Fear Itself* (see main entry, Underwood/Miller).

Index